MUSIC BEGINNERS GUIDE

Music Beginners Guide
Everything Music Students and Parents Need to Know

Jane Moyer

Copyright © New Century Leadership LLC 2014. All Rights Reserved.

No part of this publication may be reproduced, stored in a retrieval system or transmitted by any means — electronic, mechanical, photocopy, recording or otherwise — without prior permission in writing from the Publisher (except by a reviewer, who may quote brief passages in a review).

Published by New Century Leadership LLC, P.O. Box 223, Hinsdale IL 60522

Library of Congress Control Number: 2013922166
ISBN: 978-1-940975-02-3

CONTENTS

Preface: Why I Wrote This Book   *v*

Getting Started   1

Why Play Music?   3

Playing With Purpose   5

When To Begin   9

Choosing An Instrument   15

Musical Instruments   19

Popular First Instrument Choices   21

    Orchestral Strings   23

    Guitar   40

    Piano and Keyboards   46

    Woodwinds   55

    Brass   69

    Percussion   79

    Voice   83

    Folk Instruments   86

Shopping For Musical Instruments   93

Learning Partners   97

Seven Modes of Musical Learning   99

Learning Options   101

How To Choose A Private Music Teacher   104

The Suzuki Method	112
Independent Learning Programs	115
Performance Groups	117

Music Parenting   121

A Music Parent's Many Roles	123
When Your Young Musician Wants To Quit	128

Musical Development   131

Listening	133
Reading Music	137
Practicing	144
Performing	151
Musical Progress: Revisiting Your Purpose and Goals	157
Music and Careers: The Obvious and Not-So-Obvious	160
Musical Lives	164
Recommended Books	169
About The Author	175

PREFACE: WHY I WROTE THIS BOOK

Knowing my background and interest in music, friends have often come to me over the years for advice on how to get started learning music. Some were friends interested in taking up music as adults. Others were parents hoping to get their children off to a good start with music lessons. They would ask questions such as:
- *When should my child start music lessons? Or, Is it too late for me to start?*
- *Which instrument is the best to start with?*
- *Where should I go to buy an instrument? What should I look for?*
- *How can I find a good teacher?*
- *How much should I or my child be practicing?*

Soon, particularly for parents, other questions would come up, such as:
- *How do I get my child to practice?*
- *Should she join a certain band or orchestra?*
- *What should I do when he says he wants to quit?*

This book attempts to answer those questions, as well as keep you from making common mistakes I've made or witnessed over the years as a music student, music teacher and music parent.

Why I Wrote This Book

I wrote this book because *I love music.* I love listening. I love playing. I love performing. I love collaborating with other musicians. I love seeing how music enriches lives.

I also wrote this book because *I love to see people enjoy learning and growing.* I love to see the spark when learning comes together. I love to see the confidence that comes along with learning new skills. I love to see fears fade away.

I wrote this because *I've been a busy parent.* I know how hard it was to find time to do a good job investigating options for my own and my child's musical education and activities. Sorting out the choices was challenging even for one with a music background. I'd like to simplify this for other aspiring musicians and music parents.

Lastly, I'm writing this because *I'd love to save aspiring musicians and music parents from some of the mistakes I've made* and some of the most common ones I've watched others make.

Streamlining the Startup Process

My aim in sharing what I have learned is to help people interested in taking up music — either as adult beginners or music parents — streamline the startup process. Specifically, this book will help them:

- Identify musical readiness, interests and goals in order to choose a satisfying musical path
- Access basic information on musical instruments all in one place
- Select an instrument and type of music they'll want to practice
- Know where to go and what to look for when acquiring an instrument
- Sort out music learning options
- Find a teacher who will help them thrive
- Choose motivating performance opportunities
- Learn how to get better practice results with less pain
- Stay on the road to musical progress
- Recognize the full spectrum of the benefits of learning music
- Avoid common music beginner mistakes

Common Music Beginner Mistakes To Avoid

Some of the most common mistakes music beginners and music parents make are:

- Assuming there's one right path for every music student
- Failing to recognize the role of motivation in learning
- Wasting money on poor quality instruments
- Choosing a teacher who is not a good fit for the student and his or her goals
- Forcing mindless practice sessions that achieve little and can even set the learner back by reinforcing wrong notes and poor habits
- Needlessly developing or prolonging a fear of performing

Of course, I can't save you from every mistake. My suggestions may not provide perfect answers for everyone. And it isn't possible in a short book to cover every aspect of instruments and music learning. As you step onto your musical path, you'll want to call upon other experts — teachers, experienced reputable musical instrument dealers, directors of performing groups, other musicians, parents and resources — for more specific information.

Being able to play, share and appreciate music has added immeasurable joy to my life and my family's life. I realize not every family will be as crazy about music as ours, but my hope is that I can help many experience to some degree the joy of music-making and the ways learning music can enhance lives.

Where I'm Coming From

I've loved music all of my life. Early on, I sang along with my dad's records and lapped up piano lessons. I played in the school band and then joined the choir. My first job was teaching piano lessons at age 14. My parents supported my dream of earning a college degree in music, secretly hoping, I suspect, that I would "get it out of my system". After college, I did earn a masters degree and began a career in another field, but I had hardly gotten it out of my system! It turned out that not having to worry about paying the rent with my music was actually very freeing. I enjoyed serving as a church musician. I started picking up instruments that had been forbidden in music school and even hanging out with some musicians who didn't read music. I learned to play ten different instruments. I researched and wrote about opera. I performed folk music in coffee houses and festivals. I took a stab at songwriting. I connected with a jazz piano teacher and learned to play from lead sheets. I found a vocal jazz teacher who taught me to scat sing.

Shortly after I became a parent, I took some classes in making music with young children. I also took some training to become a Suzuki piano teacher. While my heart was in it, the reality of holding down a day job, moonlighting as a church musician and caring for a young child hit home quickly. I realized there was little time for that fourth job. But I also soon found that other moms who knew I was a musician were asking for advice. I loved sharing what I had learned over the years as a music student, private music teacher, performing professional, accompanist, ensemble member, sing-a-long host, and collector of musical instruments.

Being a music parent brought additional experiences and perspective. Our son chose to start on violin, dabbled on piano and later picked up trumpet and electric guitar. We became Suzuki parents, orchestra, string quartet, band, and jazz band parents. In these new roles, I learned a great deal by watching our son and others with a variety of teachers, instruments, conductors and performing organizations. I also have enjoyed accompanying middle-school and high-school musicians performing in a variety of local programs and contests.

Lastly, in recent years my "day job" shifted from business management to talent development. In working with professionals of all kinds who want to advance, I've developed expertise and tools that allow me to help them accelerate their progress by understanding their natural style and motivation, practicing effective productivity techniques, and developing their innate creativity — all of which are relevant to aspiring musicians.

Preface

As a warm-up, here are a couple of discoveries I made along the way:
- One size does not fit all. Just as kids are all different, the same musical path isn't right for everyone.
- Motivation counts.
- Learning partners — teachers, conductors, parents — make a big difference.
- Knowing what to look for when you shop for an instrument can save both money and frustration in the long-run.
- The benefits of learning music extend far beyond the music-making itself.

I'm delighted to accompany you as you begin your musical journey. Let's get started!

GETTING STARTED

WHY PLAY MUSIC?

Just as most Little Leaguers don't end up playing Major League ball, most kids (or adults) who start music lessons or join the school band, orchestra or choir, will not end up playing music professionally. Learning music does carry many immediate and lifelong benefits, however.

Fun: First, playing music is fun. (Admit it, wouldn't it be fun to be able to sit down and play your favorite song on the piano or play in a band with your buddies?)

Friends: While you make music, you're likely to make friends. Often, the other musicians you play with will become friends. You'll share the challenge and joy of performing for others. You'll connect in inexplicable ways through the beat and harmony of your sound. You may even commiserate over hard parts and the discipline required. The act of sharing your music can open the door to other new friendships as well.

Achievement: As with most worthwhile activities, learning to play music well requires energy, focus, love and discipline. The results are worth it, though. It feels great when, after much practice, the piece "plays itself."

Confidence: Realizing the results of focused work creates confidence.

Intelligence: Some neuroscience researchers have found that listening to and playing music has benefits for the brain, such as improved neural connections, intelligence and memory.

Health: Music feeds the soul. In an increasingly hurried world, playing music creates balance and relieves stress by allowing us to leave the outer world behind.

Adventure: In the course of making music, musicians get around. They have opportunities to perform in places they would probably not otherwise go — not just concert venues, but churches, retirement homes and other community spaces as well. Music groups also often have opportunities to travel — sometimes to very exciting places!

Character: Many good character qualities are developed through the experience of listening to and learning music, such as an appreciation of beauty, excellence and creativity.

Career Opportunities: A small percentage of music students will go on to pursue careers that involve music. Besides performance careers, musicians find career opportunities in areas such as teaching, composing, music-related retailing, advertising, arts administration and other creative fields.

Career Preparation: While the number of musicians who pursue a career directly related to music is small, almost all musicians find that their music background has prepared them in significant ways for success in other careers. Through music study, they have developed the discipline and focus needed to create good results. They have learned to listen well and make distinctions. They have learned to perform well both as individuals and as team members.

PLAYING WITH PURPOSE

What's your purpose for learning to play music?

There are many reasons and potential benefits to making music; they will be different for each individual, depending on their interests, goals and capabilities.

In order to achieve good progress and to persist through the inevitable challenges that come up along the way, it helps to recognize clearly *why* you are learning to play music. Not why other people do it, not why a parent or spouse or teacher wants you to do it, not why a friend or competitor is doing it, but why YOU are doing it.

Your Musical Learning Purpose

So, why do you want to learn to make music? Really. Write it here:

I want to learn to make music because...

This is your overall reason to pursue music — what you hope and intend to do with it in the long-run.

Here are some examples of Music Learning Purposes:

I want to be able to:
- ♪ Play in a rock band
- ♪ Play holiday songs for a family sing-along
- ♪ Play in the school or community orchestra
- ♪ Sing a solo in church with confidence
- ♪ Understand and appreciate what's going on when I go to the symphony
- ♪ Teach music
- ♪ Write music
- ♪ Play for or with my friends
- ♪ Play professionally
- ♪ Play at a professional level, even though I don't plan to play professionally

Your Music Learning Goals

Next, come up with specific Music Learning Goals — specific accomplishments you are aiming for within a certain timeframe on your way to fulfilling your overall musical purpose.

Specifically, I will...(do what) by...(when).

Here are some examples of specific Music Learning Goals:

My current goal is to...
- ♪ Learn how to play the guitar chords most used in folk music in two months
- ♪ Learn to play five holiday songs by Thanksgiving
- ♪ Learn scales and two contrasting pieces so I can audition for the orchestra in August
- ♪ Learn to sing with a good vibrato this year

- ♪ *Improve my technique so I can play a specific difficult piece by next year*
- ♪ *Earn a passing grade in Music Theory this semester*
- ♪ *Complete Suzuki Book 3 by the end of the year*
- ♪ *Write two songs for our rock band's next gig*
- ♪ *Play at "Open Mic" night next month*
- ♪ *Play in a recital next spring*
- ♪ *Participate in a competition next year*

You'll notice that these goals are written so that you'll know when you've reached them.

Think of the Musical Learning Purpose as your destination and your Music Learning Goals as steps along the way.

Your purpose and goals can change. In fact, it's highly likely that they will change as you learn more, hear more and experience more music. Also, your purpose may stay the same for a long time, or forever, but goals will change often. As you reach one, you will set another.

Keeping your musical purpose and goals in mind will help you stay on track and progress. It will help you determine which teacher or performing group is the right fit for you. It will help you make good choices about how you invest your time and energy. It will help you keep going when the going gets tough. It also can keep you from feeling either frustrated or superior comparing yourself to others who have different interests, goals or capabilities.

Note for Parents: Parents will usually have a goal in mind for their child when they set up music study, at least in the beginning. That is appropriate, however eventually it will really need to be the child's own purpose and goals motivating them. Very young children may be intrigued with aspects of music, but they haven't had much musical experience yet, so it is appropriate and necessary for the parent to gently guide them. As they gain more experience, they will also come up with their own ideas of what's good about music and what they'd like to be able to do. For instance, they may discover they like a certain instrument's sound or love a certain musician's style. They may find out that the middle school jazz band takes a trip to Disney World or that high school orchestra members have an opportunity to travel to New York or Europe. They might notice that rock 'n roll band members attract fans or that there are scholarships available for viola players. Their reasons may be different from yours at a certain point and it will be their own goals that keep them moving forward.

WHEN TO BEGIN

Parents often wonder when the best time is for their child to begin music lessons. They want to make sure their child is ready to benefit from the lessons, yet they don't want to miss out by having them start "too late". They may also lament that they didn't take lessons when they were young. When is too soon? When is too late?

Good news — while parents may worry that they've missed the magic moment as they watch other people's 3- or 4-year-old kids up on the stage playing an instrument, it's NEVER too late for either a child or an adult to start music lessons. And since music starts with listening, music learning has been going on since before birth.

The best time to begin formal learning depends on the individual. Are they ready physically? Are they mature enough? Are they interested? Do they have enough time and support?

One of the biggest factors is interest. Parents can take steps to cultivate their child's interest in music, but it can't be forced. It usually can't be suppressed, either! Sometimes a child will see and hear someone play a certain instrument and KNOW they must play that particular instrument, too. In other cases, the child will become interested in music by hearing someone perform on a particular instrument, but will be happy playing any instrument. It can be largely a matter of exposure, so consider ways to expose your child to a range of musical styles and instruments in ways that are fun.

Along with the interest factor, natural musicality can be a factor. Many music educators believe we are ALL naturally musical, though. The Suzuki Method, for example, is based on the theory that we can develop our natural musical abilities the same way we learn language naturally at a young age — through listening, imitation and encouragement.

Additional readiness factors include:
- Physical Size and Coordination: The student should be able to hold and play the chosen instrument without struggling.
- Maturity: The student needs to be ready to listen and follow directions.

Starting Early (Ages 4-6)

Starting early may be appropriate if you have a very musical child. Early signs of musical talent include:
- ♬ Ability to match pitches by or around age 2
- ♬ Ability to repeat back rhythms
- ♬ Ability to remember tunes
- ♬ Ability to "pick out" a tune by ear
- ♬ Frequent singing along with or repeating songs

There are benefits of starting early:
- Primary Listening Ability: Our innate listening abilities are particularly keen up to age 7.
- Natural Curiosity: Young children are natural learners.
- Fearlessness: Younger children usually haven't yet learned to be fearful about performing in front of others or making the kind of mistakes that are part of the natural learning process.
- More Time: At this age, children usually don't have a lot of competing demands from school.

Consider the following factors if you have an early starter:
- Interest: Be sure that the child is interested in music, not just the parent.
- Parent Involvement: Parents will need to be more involved in guiding younger students in their practice and musical activities.
- Teaching Methods: Make sure the teaching methods are appropriate for young children. For instance, most young children respond well to learning games and lots of encouragement. Start with shorter lessons, pieces and practice times and gradually expand them as attention span and skill increase.
- Listening: Tap into young children's keen listening sense by playing music for them often.
- Reading: It can be difficult for a child to learn to read music before or at the same time they are learning to read language. Consider the Suzuki Method for young children. The Suzuki Method guides young students to learn by listening and imitating. Suzuki students develop musical listening, coordination and tone first and then later learn to read music.
- Size: Chose an instrument that fits your child's size. Certain instruments, such as violin and guitar, are available in small sizes. Soprano recorders usually work well for young children. Start with something they can manage and upgrade the size or switch to a different instrument when they are ready.

Starting At Age 7+

Traditional music students typically start between ages 7-11. The benefits of waiting until age 7+ to begin include:
- Greater overall development in maturity, physical coordination and attention span
- A larger choice of instruments
- Established reading skill

- Availability of school support and activities, such as band
- Capability of more independent learning and practice

If beginning music study at this stage, your child:
- Will likely be taught to read music from the start. To become a good musician, it's also important to learn to develop a good "ear" by listening and being able to distinguish between and reproduce different pitches, rhythms and tones.
- May enjoy being involved with their peers in group playing, such as band, orchestra or ensemble activities.

Adolescents

What about adolescents? Is it too late to start? Of course not! Here are some issues to keep in mind:
- Older beginners may feel awkward at first around their peers who started earlier. If they are willing to practice, though, they usually can progress quickly.
- Older students usually have more specific interests than younger ones. It's important to understand and support their interests and goals — then they are usually quite motivated.
- Teenagers usually have a lot of competing demands on their time, so it may be harder to work in regular practice time.
- At this point, most could physically handle any instrument, so there is a large range of choices. Some students who started out on other instruments will switch over to or add new instruments at this stage, particularly if they have a good musical foundation and certain instruments are in demand in school or local musical groups.

Adults

It's NEVER too late to begin or to start back up again. Here are a few tips for adult music students:
- The biggest challenge for adult music students is often simply being able to find time to practice. Schedule practice time just as

you would any other important activity. If your time is limited, aim for shorter, but more frequent sessions instead of rare long ones. Be patient with yourself and persistent in working toward your goals.
- It can be a lot of fun to take lessons along with your child. You can be a good role model, too. Just don't be too upset if they start to pull ahead of you at a certain point!
- Music study provides many benefits to adults. Not only is it creatively and artistically satisfying, but it can keep your thinking sharp, relieve stress, and provide an opportunity to make new friends.

Getting Ready For Music Lessons

From the beginning, children soak in the sounds around them. Even before birth, they can recognize their mother's voice. Early on, they have a heightened ability to learn by listening. By listening and imitating sounds, they learn language naturally. Through exposure to music, singing, and expressive voices, they learn to recognize different musical tones.

Work with this natural ability. Have fun with music in your home:
- ♪ Listen to different types of music – classical, pop, folk, jazz, world music.
- ♪ Check out classical music suggested for children. Explain how some music tells a story without words, using different sounds, instruments, and themes to represent different characters and actions. Some examples:
    - ○ *Peter and the Wolf* (Prokofiev)
    - ○ *Carnival of the Animals* (Saint-Saëns)
    - ○ *The Nutcracker* (Tchaikovsky)
    - ○ *The Sorcerer's Apprentice* (Dukas)
- ♪ Dance to and act out music.

- ♪ Sing together, even if you think you don't have a good voice. (Later, your kids may become critical, but as young children, they will enjoy your songs and rhymes.)
- ♪ Take out the pots and pans and some wooden spoons and let kids "play the drums" along with the beat of songs. Tap and clap to rhythms as you listen.
- ♪ Let kids "conduct" an orchestra along with the conductor in a YouTube or other video.
- ♪ Seek out age-appropriate concerts — for example, at your library or in the park — where kids can see performers, including young ones, live. Seeing and hearing musicians live can make a big impression.

Remember that we tend to like music that is familiar to us. For example, we may like "Top 40" songs, because those were the ones played over and over on the radio. At an early age, parents are tastemakers. So use the opportunity early on to influence kids' musical choices. (Later, they'll rely on their peers for that!)

"Good music is 'beyond category'." – Duke Ellington

CHOOSING AN INSTRUMENT

Which instrument should you play? How do you decide where to start?

There are many considerations when choosing your first instrument. (Think of it as a start. If you love music, your first instrument need not be your only instrument.)

Let's look at your choice from two distinct standpoints: First, Motivational, then Practical

Motivation

Let's start with motivation: Musically speaking, what do you love?

- ♪ *What sounds (literally) good to you? What type of music interests you?* When you consider this, try to separate yourself from your neighbors and peers. Don't just consider what your friends like, what is "popular", or what is most familiar to you. Listen to and consider different types of music and sounds. What are you drawn to? If anything were possible, what type of music would you like to play?
- ♪ *Why is music important to you? What role do you want it to play in your life?* Do you like the idea of eventually playing *for* others?

Don't worry, you don't have to play in a professional orchestra or be a popular recording artist to share your music with others.

♪ *Do you like the idea of playing with others? Or do you like the idea of being able to play by yourself?* Some instruments are more naturally "social" than others. For instance, there is an abundance of solo piano material. If you learn to play the piano, you could play solo all the time, although you might also enjoy providing accompaniment for another solo instrument, small ensemble or vocal group. On the other hand, if you play an oboe or a trombone, much of the music you play will involve others, for instance, in an orchestra or band.

Start with these types of questions, because, as with anything else, getting good at music requires energy and practice. Loving the sound and the music gives you a good reason to persist.

Practical Considerations

In choosing an instrument, there are always practical considerations as well, such as cost and availability, physical fit, access to teachers, practice space and performing opportunities, maintenance requirements and natural progression from one instrument to another.

Cost and Availability

Cost is often an important consideration. It costs more to get started with some instruments than others.

You already have an instrument that doesn't cost you anything, though — your voice. You might already have an instrument at home or access to one at little or no cost through a friend or school. You might be able to rent an instrument so you can try it before you buy it. If cost is a factor, you might also consider buying a used instrument. As you become an increasingly proficient player, you are likely to want and appreciate having a "better", more expensive instrument, but you may be able to step into that gradually.

It's very important, though, to start with an instrument that is in good playing condition. If you are trying to start on an instrument that is just too cheap or in poor condition, you are likely to get frustrated and not enjoy playing.

Availability of instruments is less of an issue than it used to be, with instruments of all kinds being available through internet sites.

Physical Fit:
- ♪ Size: Some instruments are available in different sizes. For instance, violin can be an appropriate choice for a very young child, since instruments are available in sizes that fit tiny hands, while, of course, a tuba would be out of the question.
- ♪ Capability: Certain instruments make other physical demands. For example, woodwind instruments, such as flute, clarinet, or oboe, require good breath, as do brass instruments, such as trumpet or trombone. Additionally, wind and brass instruments have mouthpieces that may be difficult for some.

Where Will I Learn, Practice and Play?
- ♪ You'll need a teacher. You can teach yourself, of course, but for your first musical experience, it helps to have an experienced guide. Most people start either with a private teacher or with a group, such as a beginning band, orchestra or class. Additionally, there are now many good materials available online.
- ♪ You'll need a practice space. Personally, I like my own noise, but don't always like other people's noise. Your neighbors may feel the same way, so this could be a consideration. A keyboard with headphones for practicing could be a good choice if you're in an apartment with thin walls. If you want to learn to play the organ, you'll probably need access to a church.

♪ If you are playing a band or orchestra instrument, you'll definitely want a group to play with nearby. While you won't absolutely need access to a group to enjoy playing some other instruments, such as guitar or banjo or other folk instruments, playing with others can be very enjoyable and motivating.

Care and Feeding

Any instrument you choose will require some care and maintenance. A piano, for instance, will need to be tuned by a professional from time to time — usually at least once a year. Most stringed instruments need new strings every few months. Most woodwind instruments require a regular supply of reeds.

Transporting Your Instrument

Obviously, a flute is easier to carry around than a harp. A guitar is a better choice than a piano if you see yourself playing at the beach. If you plan to transport your instrument, consider purchasing a good quality case along with the instrument.

Your Future

Once you know how to play any instrument, learning another comes more easily.

Learning to play the piano provides an especially good foundation for learning other instruments, as it involves not only learning to coordinate between two hands (and a pedal), but also learning to read music on both the treble clef and the bass clef.

Some instruments lead naturally to others. For instance, a violin student who is motivated to do so, can often switch over to viola fairly easily. While it requires learning to read a different clef, the C clef, the technique is basically the same. Taking on the tenor sax is not so difficult if you already play the alto sax.

Now, let's explore your specific musical instrument choices.

MUSICAL INSTRUMENTS

POPULAR FIRST INSTRUMENT CHOICES

Knowing some basic information about instruments will simplify the startup process and increase the likelihood of making a satisfying choice. Here are some questions that will be addressed for popular first instruments in this section to help you make a good decision:

Instrument Basics
- ♪ How is the instrument played?
- ♪ Is it a good choice for a beginner?
- ♪ If I choose this instrument, what type of music will I play?
- ♪ If I choose this instrument, where will I play?
- ♪ What does the instrument sound like?
- ♪ Who are some famous players I can listen to?
- ♪ What are some famous pieces for this instrument I can listen to?

Learning Basics
- ♪ How will I learn to play this instrument?
- ♪ What musical opportunities might be available?
- ♪ What might be challenging?

Practical Basics:
- ♪ *What should I look for when shopping for this type of instrument?*
- ♪ *How much should I expect to invest?*
- ♪ *What else will I need?*
- ♪ *What type of care or maintenance will be needed?*

These questions are addressed separately for each instrument or instrument family so that you can move directly to the instrument choices that interest you most. This section is designed as a reference tool, so feel free to skim and skip around.

For each instrument, a list of famous players and pieces is provided. If you don't have a particular instrument in mind or if you are trying to choose between a few, you might first explore your options by doing some listening (and watching on YouTube) to see what appeals most to you.

General suggestions about shopping for musical instruments will be found at the end of this section, while specific suggestions on what to look for when shopping for each particular instrument are contained within the information for that instrument. Additionally, an attempt has been made to include some estimate of instrument cost. Prices can vary a great deal, depending on how and where you buy an instrument, as well as the extent to which accessories, setup and service are included. Please consider these sample prices as merely general estimates for perspective.

ORCHESTRAL STRINGS

The full string family includes orchestral instruments, such as Violin, Viola, Cello, and Double Bass, as well as many instruments used primarily in folk, rock or popular music, including several types of Guitars, Electric Bass, Banjo, Mandolin, Dulcimer, Autoharp, Lute and Ukulele. The string family also includes the Harp.

Sound is produced on stringed instruments by plucking, picking or drawing a bow across strings to make them vibrate.

The violin, viola, cello and double bass each have four strings. The player uses their right arm to draw a bow across the strings, usually one at a time, to make them vibrate, while pressing the fingers of the left hand down on the strings at specific points on the instrument's fingerboard to produce specific pitches. To create a different type of sound, the strings can also be plucked with a finger instead of bowed.

The other stringed instruments are plucked or picked instead of being bowed. Another important difference between the orchestral strings and most of the other stringed instruments, such as guitar, is that the fingerboards on the non-orchestral stringed instruments are marked with "frets", metal strips inserted across the fingerboard to indicate where to put down fingers to play each specific pitch.

The orchestral instruments, however, have no frets. The player needs to learn exactly where to place his or her fingers to produce the desired note, so playing them requires a good sense of pitch and coordination.

Violin

Beginning Violin

Since violins are made in a range of sizes, including very small sizes, violin is an appropriate choice for very young musicians.

Young violinists often begin by studying with teachers who teach the Suzuki method. With this method, young musicians first learn to play by listening and imitating, and then later learn to read music. Slightly older students may be able to start to learn to play through school orchestra programs. Adults usually start with private, group or online violin or fiddle lessons.

Violin Music

Violins are used in many types of music, from orchestral music, chamber music and classical solo violin music to fiddle music, bluegrass, Celtic music and even occasionally jazz.

Violinists read music on the treble clef. 𝄞

Opportunities For Violinists

Orchestras usually have more violins than any other instrument. In fact, orchestras have two violin sections, the First Violins and the Second Violins, since major composers usually wrote two different violin parts. First Violins often play the melody part, while Second Violin parts vary, sometimes including the melody or parts of it, as well as harmony and supporting parts. The orchestra's top violinist, who sits in the "first chair" in the front closest to the conductor and audience, is a type of leader whose duties include leading the tuning of the orchestra before they play.

Violinists have many other opportunities to play. String quartets include a First Violin and a Second Violin, along with a Viola and a Cello. An abundance of music has been written for solo violin,

Musical Instruments

including pieces intended to be played either without accompaniment, or accompanied by an orchestra or piano.

Violins are also often used in folk or bluegrass music, where they are called "fiddles". Additionally, violins are often used to add descant or harmony lines in many styles of music. They're even used occasionally in jazz ensembles and rock groups.

Listening: Famous Violinists

♪ Joshua Bell (classical)
♪ Jascha Heifetz (classical)
♪ Anne-Sophie Mutter (classical)
♪ Itzhak Perlman (classical)
♪ Pinchas Zukerman (classical)
♪ Natalie MacMaster (fiddle)
♪ Mark O'Connor (fiddle)
♪ Regina Carter (jazz)
♪ David Garrett (variety of styles, from classical to rock)
♪ Alison Krauss (country-bluegrass singer who also plays fiddle)

Listening: Famous Pieces That Feature The Violin

♪ Bach: Concerto for 2 Violins in D Minor, BMV 1043, 1st movement
♪ Bach: *Air on the G String*
♪ Massenet: "Meditation" from *Thais*
♪ Mendelssohn: Concerto in E Minor, 1st Movement
♪ Monti: *Czardas*
♪ Mozart: Serenade No. 13 for Strings in G Major, K. 525, *Eine Kleine Nachtmusik*
♪ Paganini: *Caprice No. 24*
♪ Vivaldi: *The Four Seasons*
♪ Charlie Daniels Band: *The Devil Went Down to Georgia*

Violin Sizes

Violins are made in several different sizes to accommodate younger students with smaller fingers. A full-sized violin is designated 4/4, while the smallest size normally available is 1/16. In between, violins are typically available in 1/10, 1/8, 1/4, 1/2 and 3/4 sizes. (Note: These sizes do not indicate literal measurements. That is, a 3/4 size violin is not literally 3/4 the length of a full-sized violin.) At a local store, the salesperson can help determine the right size. Online stores often have videos and other resources via website or phone to help with this as well. The best source of advice on which size to choose, though, can be your own teacher if you have one.

Violin Cost

Violins vary greatly in price, depending on the quality and age of the wood and the workmanship. While a very inexpensive instrument may seem like a good buy, trying to learn on a poor quality instrument can be very frustrating for students. Both good workmanship and quality of sound are important factors. It is also very important to have well-fitting tuning pegs that are easy to turn and then firmly hold the strings in tune.

Sample Prices

Beginner "Outfit"	Intermediate	Advanced
$250-$500	$600-$1,500	$2,000+

What Else You'll Need

Besides the violin itself, a violinist will need a good bow and case, as well as a shoulder rest. A violinist also needs a cake or block of rosin to rub on the hair of their bow to enable it to grip the strings and make sound. A tuner, metronome and music stand are recommended as well.

Violin Bows

Bows can range in cost from approximately $25-100 for a beginner, to $400-600 for an intermediate and $750-2,500+ for an advanced player. In addition to traditional wooden ones, bows made from synthetic materials, ranging from fiberglass to carbon-fiber, are now available. These durable synthetic bows are a good alternative for younger players. Choice of bows becomes more important as the student advances and develops techniques that produce different sounds. Bows vary in weight and flexibility, allowing for differences in dynamics and tone. By the intermediate level, most players notice differences in bows and start to develop personal preferences.

Violin Tuning

The violin will need to be tuned each time it is played. Violin strings are, from lowest to highest: G, D, A, E. Start by tuning the "A" string to a tuner, accompanying instrument, such as a piano, or designated instrument in an ensemble (usually the oboe in an orchestra). Then tune the other strings by ear in perfect fifths to that (or continue with a tuner if you are using one).

For information on violin care, see "Stringed Instrument Care and Maintenance" near the end of this chapter.

Viola

Beginning Viola

Violas have much in common with violins. They are a little larger, but they are held the same way. Violas are made in a range of sizes, including small sizes appropriate for young musicians. The smallest violas are approximately equivalent to a 1/2 size violin. (Note: Violins come as small as 1/16 size.) Violists often start first with violin and transfer to viola around age 12.

Young violists often begin by studying with teachers who teach the Suzuki method. Slightly older students may be able to start to learn to play through school orchestra programs, as well as with private teachers. Private teachers often teach both violin and viola.

Viola Music

Violas are used mainly in classical music in orchestras and chamber music. There is not as much solo music written specifically for viola as for violin, however many pieces originally written for violin, cello, clarinet, or voice have been transcribed for viola. Violas are not used as often as violins in folk and bluegrass music, however fiddling method books and ensemble pieces are available for student violists.

Violists read music on the C clef.

> **Listening: Famous Violists**
> - William Primrose
> - Lionel Tertis
> - Kim Kashkashian
> - Michael Kugel
> - Emanuel Vardi

Opportunities For Violists

The viola has a beautiful tone lower in pitch and deeper in timbre than the violin. Good violists are almost always in demand to play in orchestras, string quartets and other chamber music groups.

> *"The difference between violin and viola is that the viola is a violin with a college education".*
>
> – William Primrose, Famous Violist

> **Listening: Pieces That Feature The Viola**
> - Telemann: Viola Concerto
> - Brahms: *Two Songs for Contralto, Viola and Piano*
> - Brahms: Viola Sonatas
> - Bach: *Brandenburg Concerto No. 3*
> - Stamitz: Viola Concerto in D Major
> - Berlioz: *Harold in Italy*
> - Smetana: String Quartet No. 1, *From My Life*

Viola Sizes

Violas are made in several different sizes to accommodate younger students with smaller fingers. A full-sized viola body is 16.5″, while the smallest size normally available is 12″. In between, violas are typically available in 13″, 14″, 15″, 15.5″ and 16″ sizes. At a local store, the salesperson can help you determine the right size based on your arm length. Online stores often have videos and other resources via website or phone to help with this as well. The best source of advice on which size to choose, though, can be your own teacher if you have one.

Viola Cost

As with violins, viola prices vary widely, depending on the quality and age of the wood and the workmanship. While a very inexpensive instrument may seem like a good buy, trying to learn on a poor quality instrument can be very frustrating for students. Both good workmanship and quality of sound are important factors. It is also very important to have well-fitting tuning pegs that are easy to turn and then firmly hold the strings in tune.

Sample Prices

Beginner "Outfit"	Intermediate	Advanced
$200-500	$700-1,250	$1,500+

What Else You'll Need

In addition to the viola itself, a violist will need a good bow and case, as well as a shoulder rest. A violist also needs a cake or block of rosin to rub on the hair of their bow to enable it to grip the strings and make sound. A tuner, metronome and music stand are recommended as well.

Viola Bows

Bows can range in cost from approximately $25-100 for a beginner, to $250-700 for an intermediate and $750-2,500+ for an advanced player. In addition to traditional wooden ones, bows made from synthetic materials, ranging from fiberglass to carbon-fiber, are now available. These durable synthetic bows are a good alternative for younger players. Choice of bows becomes more important as the student advances and develops techniques that produce different sounds. Bows vary in weight and flexibility, allowing for differences in dynamics and tone. By the intermediate level, most players notice differences in bows and start to develop personal preferences.

Tuning Your Viola

The viola will need to be tuned every time it is played. From lowest to highest, the viola strings are C, G, D and A. Start by tuning the "A" string to a tuner, accompanying instrument, such as a piano, or designated instrument in an ensemble (usually the oboe in an orchestra). Then tune the other strings by ear in perfect fifths to that (or continue with a tuner if you are using one).

For information on viola care, see "Stringed Instrument Care and Maintenance" near the end of this chapter.

Cello

Beginning Cello

Cellos are made in a range of sizes, including small sizes appropriate for young musicians. Usually a student is ready for a full-size cello around age 12.

Young cellists often begin by studying with teachers who teach the Suzuki method. Slightly older students may be able to start to learn to play through school orchestra programs, as well as with private teachers.

Cello Music

Cellos are used mainly in classical music — orchestral music, chamber music and classical solo cello music.

Cellists read music on the bass clef. 𝄢

The strings on the cello are the same as on the viola, except they sound an octave lower.

Opportunities For Cellists

Cellists have the opportunity to play in orchestras and chamber music ensembles. String quartets include a Cello, along with a First Violin, Second Violin and Viola. A great amount of music has been written for solo cello, including pieces intended to be played either without accompaniment, or accompanied by an orchestra or piano. The cello has been used occasionally in pop and rock music. In recent times, cellist Yo Yo Ma has been particularly creative in expanding the range of music for cellos by collaborating with a variety of other musicians.

Cello Sizes

Cellos are made in several different sizes to accommodate younger students with smaller fingers. A full-sized cello is designated 4/4, while the smallest size normally available is 1/16. In between, cellos are typically available in 1/10, 1/8, 1/4, 1/2, 3/4 and 7/8 sizes. (Note: These sizes do not indicate literal measurements. That is, a 3/4 size cello is not literally 3/4 the length of a full-sized cello.) At a local store, the salesperson can help you determine the right size. Online stores often have videos and other resources via website or phone to help with this as well. The best source of advice on which size to choose, though, can be your own teacher if you have one.

Cello Cost

Cello prices vary widely, depending on the quality and age of the wood and the workmanship. Some less expensive cellos are made with laminate, which usually doesn't produce as good a tone, but is more durable, which can be an advantage for younger students. When

> **Listening: Famous Cellists**
> ♪ Pablo Casals
> ♪ Jacqueline Du Pré
> ♪ Pierre Fournier
> ♪ Yo Yo Ma
> ♪ Mstislav Rostropovich

shopping for a cello, pay attention to workmanship, playability and sound and avoid very inexpensive poor quality instruments. It is very important to have well-fitting tuning pegs that are easy to turn and then firmly hold the strings in tune. It is also important that the cello is set up properly so that the strings are at a proper height to avoid discomfort or buzzing of the strings.

Sample Prices

Beginner "Outfit"	Intermediate	Advanced
$500-800	$900-1,500	$2,000+

What Else You'll Need

Besides the cello itself, a cellist will need a good bow and case. The cellist will also need a chair that will allow proper posture. To keep the cello from sliding on some floor surfaces, a rubber "donut" is placed under the cello endpin. As with other bowed stringed instruments, a cellist will need a cake or block of rosin to rub on the hair of their bow to enable it to grip the strings and make sound. A tuner, metronome and music stand are also recommended.

Cello Bows

Bows can range in cost from approximately $50-200 for a beginner, to $300-700 for an intermediate and $900-2,500+ for an advanced player. Along with traditional wooden ones, bows made from synthetic materials, ranging from fiberglass to carbon-fiber, are now available. These durable synthetic bows are a good alternative for younger players. Choice of bows becomes more important as the student advances and develops techniques that produce different sounds. Bows vary in weight and flexibility, allowing for differences in dynamics and tone. By the intermediate level, most players notice differences in bows and start to develop personal preferences.

Listening: Famous Cello Pieces

- ♪ Bach: *Prelude* from Cello Suite No. 1
- ♪ Saint-Saëns: *The Swan*
- ♪ Elgar: Cello Concerto in E Minor, op. 85, 1st movement
- ♪ Dvorak: Cello Concerto in B minor, op. 104
- ♪ Bruch: *Kol Nidrei*, op. 47
- ♪ Tchaikovsky: *Variations on a Rococo Theme*
- ♪ Brahms: Double Concerto for Violin and Cello, op. 102
- ♪ Fauré: *Elégie*, op. 24
- ♪ Haydn: Cello Concerto in C Major
- ♪ Saint-Saëns: *Allegro Appassionato*, op. 43
- ♪ Popper: *Dance of the Elves*, op. 39

Cello Tuning

The cello will need to be tuned every time it is played. From lowest to highest, the strings on the cello are C, G, D and A. Start by tuning the "A" string to a tuner, accompanying instrument, such as a piano, or designated instrument in an ensemble (usually the oboe in an orchestra). Then tune the other strings by ear in perfect fifths to that (or continue with a tuner if you are using one).

For information on cello care, see "Stringed Instrument Care and Maintenance" near the end of this chapter.

Double Bass

Beginning Double Bass

The Double Bass also goes by several other names: String Bass, Contrabass, Bass Fiddle, Upright Bass. A full-sized bass is 6 feet tall from the endpin to the top of the scroll. It is played either standing up or sitting on a stool. Because of the size, it does require some height and strength to stand, hold and control, however basses are made in a range of sizes to accommodate younger musicians. The strings are large and thick and the space between notes is large, requiring frequent shifting of position, so it can be difficult for people with shorter arms and smaller hands to play.

Bass players usually pick up the instrument in their teens or later. Because of this, they often already have some experience playing another instrument. They may pick it up and learn through school orchestra programs or study with a private teacher.

Double Bass Music

Double Basses are used in many types of music, including classical music, jazz, bluegrass, rock, country, tango and folk.

Bass players read music on the bass clef. 𝄢 The double bass range is so low that its music has to be notated an octave higher than it sounds in order to fit on the bass clef.

Opportunities For Double Bass Players

Double Bass players have the opportunity to play in orchestras and chamber music ensembles, as well as in jazz ensembles, country, rock and other bands. There is not a lot of classical solo music performed on string bass, but in classical music, as in jazz and other genres, the bass provides a solid foundation for the music.

Different techniques are used in each type of music. When played in

---

Listening: Famous Double Bass Players

- ♪ Stacey Watton (classical)
- ♪ Gary Karr (classical)
- ♪ Ron Carter (jazz)
- ♪ Ray Brown (jazz)
- ♪ Charles Mingus (jazz)
- ♪ Charlie Haden (jazz)
- ♪ Edgar Meyer (classical, bluegrass)
- ♪ Stanley Clarke (fusion)
- ♪ Oscar Pettiford (jazz)

an orchestra or in chamber music, a bow is usually used. In earlier orchestral music, the bass often doubles the cello line. When basses began to be used in New Orleans jazz in the 1890s, a style was developed that used "walking" bass lines that played up and down scales to outline the underlying harmony of the piece. Later, in the 1920s and 30s, jazz players developed a "slap style", slapping the strings against the fingerboard to get more sound. In bluegrass, the string bass is usually plucked as the bassist keeps a steady beat for the group.

"If chocolate could sing, it would sound like a double bass."
– Gary Karr, famous bass player

Double Bass Sizes
Double Basses are made in several different sizes to accommodate younger students and different styles of playing. A full-sized Double Bass is designated 4/4, with smaller sizes ranging from 1/4 to 1/2, 5/8 and 3/4. At a local store, the salesperson can help you determine the right size. Online stores often have videos and other resources via website or phone to help with this as well. The best source of advice on which size to choose, though, can be your own teacher if you have one.

Double Bass Cost
Double Bass prices vary widely, depending on quality and age of the wood and the workmanship. Some less expensive basses are made with laminate, which usually doesn't produce as good a tone, but is more durable, which can be an important factor if it's being hauled around to gigs. Good workmanship and quality of the sound are important factors. It is also very important to have well-fitting tuning pegs that are easy to turn and then firmly hold the string in tune.

Sample Prices

Beginner "Outfit"	Intermediate	Advanced
$1,000–1,800	$2,000–3,000	$4,000+

Double Bass Accessories

Besides the double bass itself, a bass player will need a good bow and cases for the bass and bow. Bass players use different types of strings for different types of music; orchestral, jazz and "rock-a-billy" or "slap" strings all have slightly different sounds. A tuner and metronome are also recommended, along with a music stand and a stool to sit on at least while practicing. Some bass players also use a small cart or straps to move the bass and an endpin rest or protector. Lastly, a bass player playing with a bow will need a cake or block of rosin to rub on the hair of their bow to enable it to grip the strings and make sound.

Double Bass Bows

There are two types of double bass bows — the "French" or "overhand" bow, which is similar to the bows used with the other orchestral strings, and the broader, shorter "German" or "Butler" bow that is used in a "hand shake" position. Both types are used by orchestral players, depending on their preference. Some feel the German bow gives them more power, while some prefer the French bow, which they feel gives them better control.

Bows can range in cost from approximately $100–200 for a beginner, to $300–900 for an intermediate and $1,000+ for an advanced player. In addition to traditional wooden ones, bows made from synthetic materials, ranging from fiberglass to carbon-fiber, are now available. These durable synthetic bows are a good alternative for younger players. Choice of bows becomes more important as the student advances and develops techniques that produce different sounds. Bows vary in weight and flexibility, allowing for differences in dynamics and tone. By the intermediate level, most players notice differences in bows and start to develop personal preferences.

> **Classical Music Pieces That Feature The Double Bass**
>
> **Solos:**
> ♪ Saint Saëns: "The Elephant", from *Carnival of the Animals*
> ♪ Vanhal: Double Bass Concerto in D Major
> ♪ Dittersdorf: Double Bass Concerto
> ♪ Bottesini: *Gran Duo Concertante*
> ♪ Koussevitzky: Concerto for Double Bass
> ♪ Dragonetti: Double Bass Concerto in A Major
>
> **Chamber Pieces That Include Double Bass**
> ♪ Schubert: Piano Quintet in A Major, *Trout*, D. 667
> ♪ Mozart: Serenade in G Major, K. 525, *Eine Kleine Nachtmusik*
> ♪ Dvorak: String Quintet in G Major, op. 77
> ♪ Schubert: Octet, op. 166
> ♪ Beethoven: Septet in E-flat Major, op.20

Tuning Your Double Bass

The bass will need to be tuned every time it is played. From low to high, the strings are E, A, D and G. (Note: Some basses have a fifth string tuned to C or B.) Start by tuning the "A" string to a tuner, accompanying instrument, such as a piano, or designated instrument in an ensemble (usually the oboe in an orchestra). Then tune the other strings by ear in perfect fourths to that (or continue with a tuner if you are using one).

Stringed Instrument Care and Maintenance

Strings must be replaced every few months. It is wise to have an extra set of strings on hand at all times, as a string will break on occasion.

The "bridge" of the instrument, the part that raises the strings, should be checked and straightened often so that it stays perpendicular to the instrument. Occasional inspection and conditioning by a skilled technician is also recommended.

Stringed instruments are very sensitive to temperature changes and extremes. They should be stored with care to avoid very warm or cold temperatures. They should not, for instance, be left in the direct sun, next to a heater or in a warm or cold car or trunk. If they have been outside in colder temperatures, they should be allowed to warm up to room temperature inside the case.

Stringed instruments are also very sensitive to humidity fluctuations and extremes. Storage at humidity levels of 40-60%, or use of a "Dampit" — a device that is soaked in water and than inserted into the instrument to provide humidity — is recommended.

After playing, wipe the instrument carefully with a soft cloth to remove fingerprints and rosin.

The bow also needs good care. Be careful not to leave the bow where it can fall, be knocked down or stepped on. The horsehair on a bow shrinks and stretches with changes of humidity. To avoid damage, loosen it when not in use and then tighten it before playing. The hairs wear and occasionally break with use, so the bow also needs to be re-haired periodically — usually about twice a year.

Other Classical Strings

Harp

The harp has the largest range of any orchestral instrument. A concert harp is about 6 feet tall, weighs about 80 pounds and uses 47 strings and 7 pedals. The strings are made of nylon, gut or steel. To make it possible for the harpist to locate the desired notes, the "C" strings are red and the "F" strings are blue.

Harps are beautiful, but are not often chosen by beginning music students for several reasons. Harps are large, expensive, hard to transport, complicated to play and challenging to keep in tune. Young musicians who do start with harp almost always start with a folk harp or a "troubadour", a smaller, lighter, less expensive version of the harp that does not have pedals. Even these less expensive choices entail a fairly large investment. Folk harps generally range from $500-$2,000, troubadour harps from $3,000-$5,000, and concert harps from $10,000-$30,000 or more.

GUITAR

Beginning Guitar

Guitars are very popular first instruments — they're used in all types of music and we see and hear them everywhere.

Guitar can be a good starting instrument for kids, because some manufacturers make small-sized guitars. Beginners can start in group classes, online programs or with private lessons. The Suzuki Method is available for classical guitar.

Beginning guitar students usually learn to play chords by reading symbols. Melody and patterns are sometimes written out using guitar tablature — diagram-like notation showing the six strings and indicating where to put your fingers on the guitar neck.

Types of Guitars

There are three basic types of guitars: Acoustic, Classical and Electric. Each type has six strings, which in standard tuning are tuned from low to high (top to bottom as the guitar is held in playing position) as E, A, D, G, B, and E. Different pitches are produced by pressing down on the strings at different points on the neck. Guitars have "frets", slightly raised metal bars that go across the neck, that indicate where to place your fingers to play each note.

Acoustic Guitar

The acoustic guitar is the type of guitar used in folk, country and "mellow" blues, jazz and popular music. Standard acoustic guitars use six steel strings that are picked or strummed. This type of guitar is often used to play chords to accompany singing or other musical instruments. On this type of guitar, and the classical guitar, when the strings vibrate, the sound resonates in its hollow body.

Classical Guitar

The classical guitar looks similar to the acoustic guitar, but has several important differences. Instead of using steel strings, the classical guitar uses nylon strings, which produce a softer sound. On a classical guitar, the body is smaller and the neck is wider than on an acoustic guitar, so it requires a bigger reach. A classical guitarist uses a footstool under one foot to raise the guitar to a comfortable playing position. Classical guitar repertoire includes early music originally written for lute and Spanish music, as well as other pieces that have been transcribed for guitar. It is played as a solo instrument, as well as in smaller classical music ensembles. Occasionally it is featured in orchestra concertos or opera pieces.

Electric Guitar

Electric guitars are used mainly in rock music, but also in some blues, jazz and pop music, where the guitar player often gets to play "lead", a melody or solo part, as well as chords. In contrast to acoustic and classical guitars, which have sound holes and hollow bodies, electric guitars have flat, solid bodies. When the strings vibrate, the signal is picked up by wire-wrapped magnets under each string. The signal is turned into an electric current, which travels through cables to an amplifier to make the sound audible. Controls on the guitar and amplifier adjust volume, tone and effects.

Which Type of Guitar Should You Choose?

Each type has a few benefits and a few downsides. It's most important to choose the type of guitar that fits the type of music you want to play. Most beginners choose either acoustic, if they like that sound, or electric if they want to play rock. The acoustic is a bit harder at first for some beginners because the thicker strings are a little harder to press down. Beginning acoustic players soon develop small calluses on their fingertips and get used to this, though. The nylon strings on a classical guitar are easier to press down, but the wider neck can make it more difficult for those with smaller hands. An electric guitar is a little easier for a beginner to play, because the body and neck are smaller and the lighter strings are easier to press down. It does require an amplifier and cables, though, which increases the cost and complications. If you start on one type and want to switch to another later, it will be quite easy, as the notes and fingerings are the same.

Two More Types of Guitars

12-String Guitar: The 12-string guitar is an acoustic guitar that has each of the standard 6 strings doubled to make a fuller sound.

Electric Bass Guitar: The electric bass guitar, also called the "electric bass", looks similar to an electric guitar, but only has four strings, which are tuned the same as an acoustic double bass. It is used to lay down a harmonic foundation and beat in rock and other pop styles.

Guitar Sizes

It's important to get a guitar that is the right size so that it is easy to hold and play. Some guitar manufacturers make smaller sized guitars that work well for kids approximately ages 5-10. A 1/2-size guitar is about 30" and a 3/4-size guitar is 34-36". A guitar shop can help you choose the best size.

Shopping For a Guitar

The most important factors in selecting a first guitar are:
- ♪ **Type**: Choosing the type of guitar — acoustic, classical or electric — for the genre of music you want to play
- ♪ **Playability and Feel**: Is it the right size? Can you reach comfortably around the neck to play it?
- ♪ **Keeping in Tune**: Pay attention to the tuners, because it is very important to have good ones that hold the strings in tune.
- ♪ **Sound**: Do you like the sound?

Tips For Buying an Acoustic Guitar

One of the major factors that determines the price of a guitar is the type of material used in its construction. Acoustic guitars are made from wood. Less expensive models may be made of laminate (plywood), while better guitars are made of solid wood. Laminate is less expensive, but more durable, while solid wood will produce a better sound. The guitar top, sides and back may all be made of solid wood, or just the top may be solid wood. The type of wood used also will affect the cost of the instrument, as well as the type of tone. Sitka spruce is often used for solid wood acoustic guitar tops and the back and sides are usually made of some type of hardwood. The quality of construction and workmanship will also affect the price.

As with buying any instrument, it's usually best to stay away from the very cheapest instruments, as they are often very poorly constructed and playing them turns out to be frustrating. Pay attention to the sound and feel of the instrument, as well as the construction, condition and price.

If possible, have a teacher or experienced guitar player check the instrument for you. Check to be sure the neck is straight. Be sure the frets are even and not varying in height. If played properly, you shouldn't hear buzzing or rattling sounds.

Listening: Famous Guitar Players

Classical Guitar:
- ♪ Julian Bream
- ♪ Christopher Parkening
- ♪ Andrés Segovia

Country/Folk:
- ♪ "Doc" Watson
- ♪ Chet Atkins
- ♪ Hank Williams
- ♪ Merle Travis

Jazz:
- ♪ Django Reinhardt
- ♪ Wes Montgomery
- ♪ Les Paul
- ♪ Earl Klugh
- ♪ George Benson
- ♪ Pat Metheny

Blues:
- ♪ Robert Johnson
- ♪ Leadbelly
- ♪ Freddie King
- ♪ Lonnie Johnson
- ♪ Muddy Waters
- ♪ Buddy Guy
- ♪ BB King

Rock/Pop:
- ♪ Chuck Berry
- ♪ Jimi Hendrix
- ♪ Eric Clapton
- ♪ Frank Zappa
- ♪ Jeff Beck

Tips For Buying An Electric Guitar

If you're buying your first electric guitar, consider buying a "starter pack", since you will need an amp, cables, strap, picks, case and other accessories that are often bundled with it at a good price.

Check the pickups to make sure each string has the same volume level. Make sure there are no shorts, crackles or noise. Check to be sure the volume and tone controls work.

Guitar Accessories: What Else You'll Need

You'll need a case to protect your guitar. A good hardshell case is necessary if you plan to travel with it by plane or take it out to gigs or anywhere it might experience rough treatment. Otherwise, a "gig bag", or soft case may be adequate.

Some guitar players like to use a stand for the guitar when they take a break. If you use one, make sure it is sturdy.

If you will be playing standing up, you will need a strap to hold the guitar.

You'll need an extra set of strings, of course. A string winder is an inexpensive tool that will make the string-changing job easier.

For acoustic or electric guitars, you'll need a variety of picks. Use a thin flat pick for strumming and a thick one for playing individual notes. Acoustic players also use fingerpicks.

An electronic tuner is highly recommended.

Electric guitar players will also need an amplifier and cables to be able to hear the guitar. If you'd like to be able to practice quietly without disturbing others, consider buying a headphone amp as well.

Lastly, a music stand and metronome are recommended for all instrumentalists.

Guitar Care and Maintenance

Protect your guitar by keeping it in a good case.

Your guitar will need to be tuned each time before you play it. Students are usually taught how to tune the guitar by ear, but an electronic tuner is handy.

When you are done playing, wipe the strings and body with a clean soft cotton cloth to remove fingerprints and oils. Guitar strings need to be changed every few months when they start to lose their tone or become discolored and brittle. Be sure to use strings that are an appropriate gauge for your instrument. It's usually best to replace the whole set, removing and replacing one string at a time.

Since acoustic and classical guitars are made of wood, they are sensitive to temperature and humidity changes and extremes, which can cause warping, cracks in the finish, or weakening of glued joints. Keep your guitar out of direct sunlight and avoid keeping it in either very warm or cold temperatures. If it has been out in the cold, let it warm up in the case before playing it. Try to keep it at a constant humidity level, ideally between 45-55%.

PIANO AND KEYBOARDS

Beginning Piano

Piano is considered by many to be the best instrument to learn for a solid overall musical foundation. It has the greatest pitch range of any instrument, so playing the piano requires learning to read music on both treble and bass clefs. Since many notes can be played at the same time, pianists develop good coordination. Students with a good keyboard background often find it relatively easy to learn other instruments. Because the piano involves using a full musical range, keyboard facility is also useful for aspiring composers and conductors. Music schools generally require some piano proficiency for most students, particularly vocal music students.

Young pianists can start with either Suzuki method or traditional teachers. Online programs are also available. They can start with either a standard 88-key acoustic piano, or a regular-sized or slightly smaller keyboard.

Piano Music

The piano is used in a wide range of musical styles, including classical, jazz, pop, and rag. Electronic keyboards expand the range and sound possibilities.

Opportunities For Pianists

Pianists often play as soloists, but also have opportunities to play with other musicians in small groups, such as chamber music groups or jazz ensembles. Additionally, they have opportunities to provide accompaniment for other solo instruments, as well as choral and other groups.

Pianos vs. Keyboards: Acoustic vs. Electronic

Beginners have several choices to make when deciding on an instrument. The first is whether to buy a traditional acoustic piano or an electronic keyboard.

> **Listening: Famous Classical Pianists**
>
> ♪ Vladimir Horowitz
> ♪ Van Cliburn
> ♪ Vladimir Ashkenazy
> ♪ Artur Rubinstein
> ♪ Andre Watts
> ♪ Maurizio Pollini
> ♪ Mitsuko Uchida
> ♪ Wanda Landowska
> ♪ Emanuel Ax
> ♪ Alfred Brendel
> ♪ Evgeny Kissin
> ♪ Marc-André Hamelin
> ♪ Alicia de Larrocha
> ♪ Martha Argerich
> ♪ Lang Lang
> ♪ Katia and Marielle Labèque

Benefits of buying an acoustic piano include these:
- ♪ Acoustic pianos are beautiful and create a "real" sound.
- ♪ All acoustic pianos have a full range of 88 keys.
- ♪ Keys are "touch sensitive". Players usually like the "feel" and responsiveness of an acoustic instrument.
- ♪ A good quality, well-maintained piano will usually hold its value well.

There can be many benefits, though, especially to beginners, of starting with a keyboard:
- ♪ Although an inexpensive keyboard may not have a full range of keys, great sound quality or advanced features, beginners can get started for a smaller investment.
- ♪ Headphones can be used for quiet practicing.

- ♪ Many are portable and take up less space.
- ♪ While they can break and do require batteries or electricity, generally care and maintenance is less, since they don't require regular tuning.
- ♪ Some are capable of playing a variety of sounds or even different sounds on different parts of the keyboard, which can be really fun.

> **Listening: Famous Jazz Pianists**
>
> - ♪ Scott Joplin
> - ♪ Jelly Roll Morton
> - ♪ Fats Waller
> - ♪ Art Tatum
> - ♪ Oscar Peterson
> - ♪ Dave Brubeck
> - ♪ Bill Evans
> - ♪ Errol Garner
> - ♪ Keith Jarrett
> - ♪ Herbie Hancock
> - ♪ Thelonius Monk

Piano Basics

Before the piano was invented, keyboard players played the harpsichord. On a harpsichord, the strings are plucked, making a soft sound. Harpsichord-maker Bartolomeo Cristofori invented a new instrument with strings that are hit with "hammers" in 1709. This made it possible to produce either soft or loud sounds — thus the name "pianoforte", which means "soft loud" in Italian.

How it works:
- A piano has 88 keys, arranged in a regular black and white pattern.
- When a key is pressed down, it triggers a hammer to "hit" strings that then vibrate. The vibration, and therefore sound, is stopped by "dampers" that mute the strings.
- The piano has three pedals. The most frequently used pedal is the one on the right, the sustain pedal, which raises all the dampers, allowing the strings to continue to vibrate after the keys are released.

Shopping For a Piano

Piano buyers first need to decide on the type and size of instrument. There are two types of pianos:

- ♪ **Grand Pianos:** On a grand piano, the strings run parallel to the ground. Because the strings are longer than on other types of pianos, it's possible to make a louder sound. Additionally, the lid of the piano can be opened to allow more sound. Grand pianos come in several sizes. The exact lengths vary by brand and model, but generally they are:
    - Baby Grand: 5'0"-5'5"
    - Mid-sized Grand: 5'6"-6'5"
    - Large or "Semi-Concert" Grand 6'6"-8'0"
    - Concert Grand: Usually 9'0"
- ♪ **Vertical Pianos:** These piano have strings that run vertically, allowing the instrument to be placed upright against a wall, taking up less space. This category includes Spinet, Console, Studio and Upright pianos. The main difference between these types is the vertical height, ranging from the lowest, the spinet, at 36-38" high, to the upright, which can be 50-60" high.

Grand pianos generally produce the best sound, but cost more and take up more space.

As with shopping for any type of instrument, it's best to stick with quality brands for both quality and potential resale purposes. Even within brands, models and individual instruments vary, but generally, some of the best are: Steinway, Baldwin, Yamaha and Kawai. Choosing a piano, though, is also a matter of individual taste. There is a great deal of difference in tone and touch between brands and individual instruments. When shopping, try out (or have someone who plays try out) the same pieces on different instruments. Listen to the sound in every range — high, middle, and low. Consider the "touch".

Used pianos can be a good value. As with a new instrument, check out the sound and touch. Consider the overall condition and check to be sure all the keys work. If you are seriously considering a used piano, hire a piano technician to check it out for you.

> **Listening: Famous Composers' Piano Works**
>
> ♪ Bach: *Well-Tempered Clavier*
> ♪ Mozart: Sonatas
> ♪ Beethoven: Sonatas, Concertos
> ♪ Schubert: Impromptus
> ♪ Chopin: Waltzes, Ballades, Nocturnes
> ♪ Liszt: Concertos, Hungarian Rhapsodies
> ♪ Brahms: Intermezzos, Waltzes, Rhapsodies
> ♪ Debussy: Preludes, Arabesques, *Suite Bergamasque*
> ♪ Rachmaninoff: Concertos, *Rhapsody on a Theme of Paganini*, Preludes
> ♪ Gershwin: *Rhapsody in Blue*
> ♪ Mendelssohn: *Songs Without Words*
> ♪ Schumann: *Scenes from Childhood*
> ♪ Scott Joplin: *Maple Leaf Rag*, *The Entertainer*

Piano Accessories: What Else You'll Need

You'll need a good lamp and piano bench.

A bench that allows you to adjust the height is ideal. It should be adjusted for each individual so that when playing, their hands and forearms are parallel to the ground.

Some piano benches have other benefits, such as storage or width that allows for two players, but proper height should be the priority.

Piano Care and Maintenance

Keep your piano away from heat, direct sunlight, drafts or dampness. It is best not to place it on an outside wall. Keep food and drink away from it.

Wipe the keys with a damp cloth. Check the manufacturer's instructions regarding care of the outside.

Piano Tuning and Repair

With regular use, a piano should be tuned every 6-12 months. The cost of piano tuning varies by market, but will probably be in the $80-100 range. If you don't have a piano tuner already, your teacher, school or piano dealer will likely be able to recommend one.

Most piano tuners are also able to make common adjustments and repairs, such as adjusting pedals or fixing sticking keys. A specialized piano technician may be needed for certain types of unusual or infrequent repairs, such as replacement of hammers, dampers or strings or dealing with a cracked soundboard.

Piano Movers

If you need to move your piano, hire qualified movers who specialize in moving pianos if at all possible. It is worth the extra trouble and investment. They will have special equipment, a piano board. Ask your piano dealer for a recommendation if you need help finding piano movers.

Shopping for a Keyboard

Sorting out choices among the many available types of keyboards can seem daunting. Many fun and exciting features are available. So as not to be overwhelmed by the choices, consider first your budget and the types of features you are likely to want and actually use.

When considering your options, here are a few factors to use as a starting-point:

- ♪ **Use:** How do you plan to use your keyboard? Most beginners want and need a basic keyboard mainly for practicing and playing. They may enjoy a few extra fun features, but are not likely to need or use many of the advanced ones that are available. Some musicians are also looking for features that will allow them to perform using a variety of sounds. Others intend to use the keyboard for recording and editing or connecting to and controlling other instruments.

♪ **Size/Range:** Keyboards vary in size. Some versions have the standard 88 piano keys, while more portable versions usually have fewer keys, with common sizes having 25, 33, 48, 61 or 76 keys. Anything less than 61 keys will be quickly frustrating to a piano student. A 61-key keyboard can be convenient for carrying around and some practicing, but most committed students will eventually want a full-sized keyboard.

♪ **Portability:** Do you need to be able to move the keyboard often? Some keyboards are much lighter and easier to transport than others.

♪ **Touch:** "Touch sensitive" keys give you the ability to produce either soft or loud sounds. This is an important feature for developing musical playing. "Weighted" keys simulate the weighted feel of keys on an acoustic piano. While not crucial at the very beginning, this feature will be important as a student works to develop good technique.

♪ **Sounds:** Are you mainly interested in playing with a piano sound, or do you want a keyboard with a variety of sounds? How many different sounds are you likely to use? How "real" do you need those sounds to be?

♪ **Speakers:** Smaller keyboards often come with built-in speakers, while more advanced versions often require connection to a separate speaker, which makes higher quality sound possible.

Key features for beginners to consider, then, are:

♪ **Number of keys:** At least 61, and preferably 76 or 88
♪ **Touch:** Touch sensitivity, and preferably weighted keys
♪ **Sounds:** A good piano sound
♪ **Speakers:** A built-in speaker or separate speaker will be needed.

Try out various types of keyboards. Consider:

♪ *How is the sound quality?*
♪ *Do you like the preprogrammed sounds?*
♪ *How do the keys feel?*
♪ *What features are you really likely to use?*

Keyboard Options

Examples of some of the many features available on keyboards are:

- ♪ **Sounds**: Most keyboards have some variety of sounds available. Some use "sampling" to store sounds produced from recordings of the real instrument into its memory chips, while others "synthesize" sounds by imitating instruments through changing the shape of the waveform. Some allow the player to edit the sounds or manipulate them with knobs, "benders" or built-in effects, such as "delay" (echo), "reverb" or "chorus".
- ♪ **Music rack**
- ♪ **Foot Pedals**: Built-in pedals or the ability to connect an external pedal.
- ♪ **Auto-accompaniment**: This feature found on many home keyboards fills in preset rhythms and harmonies when you play a melody and/or chord.
- ♪ **Multi-timbral**: This feature allows you to play more than one sound at a time.
- ♪ **Multi-note polyphony**: This indicates how many notes you can play at once. Unless you plan to use the keyboard as a controller, for recording or other advanced purposes, 8–10 should be sufficient.
- ♪ **MIDI-capability**: MIDI stands for Musical Instrument Digital Interface. This allows you to connect and play multiple keyboards from one "controller" keyboard, as well as allowing you to "record" to a sequencer.
- ♪ **Digital recording or sequencing**: Multi-track recording allows you to record more than one track. Consider the storage size and type.
- ♪ **USB connectivity**: This allows you to connect the keyboard directly to your computer.
- ♪ **Display**: Some keyboards display information about the features and sounds you are using. Size and readability can vary quite a bit.

What Else You'll Need

Keyboard players will also need a stand, a bench, possibly a surge protector and a case if it will be transported. Your keyboard stand should be adjustable to the desired height. Some can accommodate multiple keyboards or components. If your keyboard didn't come with them, you'll probably want an external foot pedal and a rack or stand to hold your music.

Keyboard Care and Maintenance

Register your purchase. See the manufacturer's instructions for care and availability of tech support.

WOODWINDS

The woodwind family includes Flute, Piccolo, Clarinet, E-flat Clarinet, Bass Clarinet, Oboe, English Horn, Bassoon, Contrabassoon, Saxophones and Recorders.

    Woodwind instruments are not all made of wood, but they do all rely on wind to produce sound. They are played by blowing into or across a mouthpiece, which causes air to vibrate inside a narrow pipe. The player produces different pitches as the length of the vibrating pipe is changed by pressing down keys or covering holes in the instrument. Some woodwinds are actually made of wood, while others are made of metal, plastic or some combination of materials. Each instrument has a different type of sound, depending on the length of the pipe, the material it is made of, the shape and the way it is blown. Some, such as clarinet, oboe and saxophone, use a reed, a small piece of cane inserted into the mouthpiece that vibrates when the player blows on it, while players blow directly into or across the mouthpiece of others, such as recorder or flute.

    Beginners usually start with recorder, flute, clarinet or alto saxophone, but woodwind players often end up playing more than one woodwind instrument. Several use similar sound production techniques and some even share the same fingerings.

Woodwind instruments are used in orchestras and wind ensembles, as well as in many types of bands, including concert bands, marching bands, and jazz bands.

Woodwinds in Orchestras

The size of an orchestra and the exact instrumentation will vary according to the type of music being played, the era in which it was written and the preferences of the composer. Typically, an orchestra will include 2 flutes, a piccolo, 2 oboes, an English horn, 2 clarinets and 2 bassoons. Orchestral woodwind players often play more than one instrument.

Flute

Beginning Flute

Flute is a popular instrument for beginning musicians, because it is relatively uncomplicated, easy to transport, versatile and has a beautiful sound.

While early flutes, and many types of flutes used in world music, are wooden, the flutes used in orchestras today are metal — usually made of silver or silver-plate. The flute is played by blowing across a mouthpiece while holding the instrument out to the side. It consists of three parts — the head, the middle and the foot. Different pitches are produced by holding down different configurations of thirteen keys, which changes the length of the column of air vibrating inside the flute. The tone can also be altered by changing the shape of the embouchure (the shape and position of the lips), the amount of breath, and the angle at which it's blown across the mouthpiece.

The player needs to have long enough arms and large enough fingers to hold the instrument and reach the keys easily. As with all of the woodwinds, a flutist needs good breath capacity. Because the flute is held out to the side where the player can't see their fingers, it also requires good coordination. The flute is easier to play with braces on the teeth than other woodwinds. Young flutists often start playing around age 9 or 10 in a band program. Younger students may start with Suzuki method or other private teachers. Some online lessons are also available.

There are a few alternatives if a young child isn't big enough to handle a regular-sized flute comfortably. If starting early, they might start with a recorder, which gives them an opportunity to develop finger coordination and use of their breath. Some flutes are made shorter for small musicians by curving the mouthpiece around. A few instrument makers also manufacture special shorter and lighter "beginners flutes".

> **Listening: Famous Flutists**
>
> ♪ James Galway
> ♪ Jean-Pierre Rampal
> ♪ Marcel Moyse
> ♪ Emmanuel Pahud
> ♪ Ian Clarke
> ♪ Ian Anderson (rock)

Flute Music

The flute is used in many types of music. In addition to being played as a solo instrument, the flute is played in orchestras, bands, flute choirs and jazz ensembles. The flute often plays the melody in ensembles, as well as harmony descant parts that soar above the melody.

Flutists read music on the treble clef.

Opportunities for Flutists

Because the fingering is the same, experienced flutists often also play the piccolo. The piccolo is a short flute, about a foot long, that produces a very high pitch that stands out high above the rest of the instruments. "Piccolo" means "little" in Italian. It comes in two pieces.

Although it's held differently, the flute also has similar fingering to the saxophone, so that's usually an easy crossover instrument for flutists.

Listening: Famous Pieces That Feature Flute

Flute Solos
- ♪ Rimsky-Korsakov: *The Flight of the Bumblebee*
- ♪ Debussy: *Syrinx* (*La Flute de Pan*)
- ♪ Briccialdi: *Carnival of Venice*
- ♪ Chaminade: Concertino for Flute and Piano
- ♪ Fauré: *Fantasie*, op. 79
- ♪ Bach: *Badiniere* from Orchestral Suite No. 2 in B minor, BWV 1067
- ♪ Mozart: Flute Concerto in D Major, K. 314
- ♪ Bach: Partita in A minor, BWV 1013
- ♪ Poulenc: Flute Sonata
- ♪ Prokofiev: Flute Sonata in D

Orchestral Pieces That Feature Flute
- ♪ Grieg: *Peer Gynt Suite No. 1*, Op. 46, "Morning"
- ♪ Gluck: *Orfeo ed Euridice*, "Dance of the Blessed Spirits"
- ♪ Bizet: *L'Arlésienne Suite No. 2*, Menuet
- ♪ Bizet: Entr'act from *Carmen*
- ♪ Debussy: *L'apres-midi d'un faune* (Prelude to the Afternoon of a Faun)

Listening: Piccolo

- ♪ Sousa: *Stars and Stripes Forever*
- ♪ Bizet: *L'Arlésienne Suite No. 2*, Farandole

Shopping For a Flute

Resist the temptation to buy a very inexpensive flute. In the long-run, good design and construction will be worth the extra investment. It's best to stick with a good quality brand-name, such as Pearl, Jupiter, Yamaha or others. Check out your options with a teacher or an experienced player if possible before you buy. Used flutes are often available at good prices. That may be a good beginner solution, but do have the instrument checked by someone knowledgeable, because repairs or repadding can be expensive. Professional-level flutes are often silver, but that's not necessary for a student flute — most are silver-plated. Most advanced players play "open hole" flutes, but most beginners start with closed hole (plateau) flutes.

Sample Flute Prices

Beginner	Intermediate	Advanced
$300-700	$500-$1,500	$2,000+

What Else You'll Need
Be sure to get a good case to protect the flute. A music stand and metronome are recommended for all instrumentalists.

Flute Care and Maintenance
Tune the flute first when playing with other instruments by pulling the head joint out or pushing it in to increase or decrease the length of the instrument.

When putting the flute together, hold only the non-keyed parts. Never force the pieces together. Don't oil or grease the joints. If the joints are too tight or too loose, take it to a flute repair specialist for adjustment.

After playing, clean the inside of each of the three flute parts. Insert a corner of a cotton cloth through the slit at the end of a cleaning rod, wrap the cloth around the rod, insert it into the flute and turn it several times. This will remove moisture that might cause tarnishing or problems with swollen pads that don't fit well. Wipe the outside with a clean cotton cloth. Don't use any oils or liquid silver polish.

Keep the flute in a good case. Don't keep the moist cleaning cloth or other things that might damage the flute with it in the case.

Once a year or so, take the flute to a reputable repair shop for servicing. They will inspect, clean and oil the instrument, adjust keys and replace pads if needed.

Clarinet

Beginning Clarinet

The clarinet is a very popular first instrument because of its convenient size and musical versatility.

The clarinet has five parts: the mouthpiece, the barrel, the upper joint, the lower joint and the bell. The joints that hold the pieces together are lined with cork so they will fit together securely. The clarinet is played by blowing into a reed that is clipped to the mouthpiece. Different pitches are produced on the clarinet by covering and uncovering its holes in different configurations, which changes the length of the column of air vibrating inside.

As with any woodwind instrument, is important to develop good breath control and a good embouchure (the shape of the mouth around the mouthpiece). Beginners often start clarinet around age 9 or 10 in a school band or at any age with a private teacher. Some online learning programs are also available.

Clarinet Music

In addition to being played as a solo instrument, the clarinet is played in orchestras, concert, marching and jazz bands and wind ensembles.

Clarinetists read music on the treble clef.

The clarinet is a transposing instrument. That is, music written out for clarinet is transposed — raised or lowered — to a different "key". As a result, the note played sounds as a different note than the note written on the page of printed music. This is done so that the fingerings can be the same on different-sized instruments of similar design. Players of these instruments, then, can switch between similar instruments without learning new fingerings.

The clarinet is a B-flat transposing instrument. When a clarinetist reads a "C" on the page of music and fingers the note as "C" on the instrument, it sounds as "B-flat", a step lower. Clarinetists and players of other transposing instruments become accustomed to this practice. What this means, though, is that a flutist or pianist or violinist (all non-transposing instruments) cannot play along with the clarinetist using the same piece of printed music.

Opportunities for Clarinetists
Clarinetists often play several instruments. In addition to the standard B-flat clarinet, clarinets come in a few other sizes, such as the smaller, higher E-flat clarinet and the larger, lower bent-necked bass clarinet, which uses the same fingerings as the standard clarinet, but sounds an octave lower. Some orchestral pieces require the clarinetist to play more than one type of clarinet within the same piece.

There are also many similarities between clarinet and saxophone, so clarinetists often pick that up as well.

> **Listening: Famous Clarinetists**
>
> **Classical:**
> ♪ Richard Stoltzman
> ♪ Sabine Meyer
> ♪ Larry Combs
> ♪ Karl Leister
> ♪ Martin Frost
>
> **Big Band & Jazz:**
> ♪ Benny Goodman
> ♪ Woody Herman
> ♪ Artie Shaw
> ♪ Eddie Daniels
> ♪ Pete Fountain
> ♪ Johnny Dodds
> ♪ Sidney Bechet
> ♪ Paquito d'Rivera

Shopping For a Clarinet
Resist the temptation to buy a very inexpensive clarinet. Very cheap instruments are often not constructed well, which may make them hard to play or require expensive adjustments or repairs. For the long-run, it's best to stick with a good brand-name.

Most clarinets are made of wood, however some beginner models are plastic. The wood provides a warmer, better tone, but plastic is less expensive and more durable, which may make it a good choice for a younger beginner. If you buy a less expensive instrument, consider upgrading to a better mouthpiece, as that will make it easier to play.

If possible, have a teacher or an experienced clarinetist check and play the instrument (using their own mouthpiece) you are considering before you buy it. Check to be sure none of the keys are bent, no joints are loose, and that no pads are loose or missing. Listen to the tone in both the high and low registers.

Sample Clarinet Prices

Beginner	Intermediate	Advanced
$300-$700	$800-$1,500	$1,600+

Listening: Famous Classical Music Pieces Featuring Clarinet

♪ Mozart: Clarinet Concerto in A Major, K. 622
♪ Gershwin: *Rhapsody in Blue* (beginning)
♪ Offenbach: *Orpheus in the Underworld*, Overture (beginning)
♪ Prokofiev: *Peter and the Wolf* (Cat)
♪ Brahms: Sonata No. 1 in F Minor and Sonata No. 2 in E-flat Major, op. 120
♪ Weber: Clarinet Concerto No. 1 in F Minor, op. 73
♪ Weber: Clarinet Quintet op. 34
♪ Debussy: *Rhapsody for Clarinet*

What Else You'll Need

A good case, music stand and metronome are recommended for all instrumentalists. Clarinetists will also need reeds, a reed guard, a cleaning swab and cork grease.

Reeds come in different grades according to strength. Stronger, harder reeds carry higher numbers. Most beginners use softer reeds, such as a "2", and then move to stronger reeds, which produce a better tone, as they progress.

Clarinet Care and Maintenance
Tune the clarinet first when playing with other instruments by pulling the mouthpiece out or pushing it in to increase or decrease the length of the instrument.

Assemble the clarinet carefully. Put it together without putting pressure on the keys, so you don't bend or damage them. When needed, use cork grease so that the parts will connect easily. Apply a small amount and rub it around the cork. Never force the parts together. After playing, use a clean cotton cloth to wipe out the mouthpiece. Remove the moisture inside the instrument with a pull-through cotton cleaning swab. Wipe each joint. Remove the reed from the mouthpiece and store it in a reed guard.

Keep your clarinet in a good case. To prevent damage, don't keep music or anything other than small accessories in your case with it. Wooden clarinets are sensitive to temperature and humidity changes, so they should be kept out of direct sunlight or extreme temperatures. If your clarinet has been in the cold, let it warm up in the case before playing it. In dry climates or during the winter, keep a humidifier, such as a "Dampit", in the case. To prevent cracking, wooden clarinets may require a break-in period of light use to gradually absorb the type of moisture that occurs with playing.

If you have bent keys, cracks, corks that are too tight or too loose, pads that need to be replaced, or other problems, take the clarinet to a reputable technician for repairs.

Saxophone

Beginning Saxophone
The saxophone is a popular instrument for beginning musicians because of the appeal of its music, its cool appearance and its relative simplicity. It is usually easier to get a decent tone on the sax in the

beginning than on other woodwinds. The fingering is the same from one octave to another, so it is relatively simple to learn to play.

There are four common saxophone sizes – soprano, alto, tenor and baritone. Most beginners start on the alto saxophone, because the size is more comfortable for younger players and it also requires a little less breath to play than the larger tenor and baritone saxophones.

Listening: Famous Saxophonists

- ♪ Sidney Bechet (soprano)
- ♪ John Coltrane (tenor, soprano, alto)
- ♪ Ornette Coleman (alto)
- ♪ Paul Desmond (alto)
- ♪ Cannonball Adderly (alto)
- ♪ Johnny Hodges (alto)
- ♪ Art Pepper (alto)
- ♪ Benny Carter (alto)
- ♪ Charlie Parker (alto)
- ♪ Coleman Hawkins (tenor)
- ♪ Stan Getz (tenor)
- ♪ Lester Young (tenor)
- ♪ Harry Carney (baritone)
- ♪ Gerry Mulligan (baritone)

Saxophone Music

When the saxophone was patented by Adolphe Sax in 1846, it was used in military bands. Originally, there were 14 different saxophone sizes! By the 1920s, the sax was being added to dance bands, and by the 1940s, big bands typically included 2 alto saxophones, 2 tenor saxophones and 1 baritone sax, with the alto and tenor often playing solos. Saxophones are now used mostly in jazz, concert and marching bands, but occasionally a composer includes saxophone in an orchestra piece. Saxophone players read music on the treble clef, even though the tenor and baritone sax sound more than an octave below the written notation.

The saxophone is a transposing instrument. That is, music written out for sax is transposed – raised or lowered – to a different "key". Because of this, the note played sounds as a different note than the note written on the page of printed music. This is done so that the fingerings can be the same on different-sized instruments of similar design. As a result, a flutist or pianist or violinist (all non-transposing instruments) cannot play along with the saxophone player using the same piece of printed music.

The soprano and tenor saxophones, for example, are "B-flat" transposing instruments. When a player reads a "C" on the page of music and fingers the note as "C" on the instrument, it sounds as "B-flat", a step lower. The alto and baritone saxophones are E-flat transposing instruments.

Opportunities for Sax Players

Because saxophone players learn fingerings that are similar to the fingerings on the flute and on other types of saxophones, they often play several different instruments. The clarinet is also a common crossover instrument for sax players.

Shopping For a Saxophone

The cost of a sax will depend on the quality of the materials used, amount of handwork, quality of detailing, quality of tone, intonation and responsiveness.

Most saxophones today are made of brass and finished with a protective coating of clear lacquer. Different colored lacquers are available that change the appearance, but don't affect the tone. Some vintage models, as well as some new ones, may have silver, nickel, gold or other plating that may also give them a different tone.

When buying a saxophone, consider the workmanship, tone and feel. Examine the pads to make sure they cover the holes completely and are soft to the touch. Resist the temptation to buy a very inexpensive instrument.

Used instruments can often be a good value. Have a teacher or experienced player check the instrument for you to be sure it is in good playing condition, because repairs can be expensive. Watch out for dents and resoldering. Check the condition of the pads.

Sample Saxophone Prices

Beginner	Intermediate	Advanced
$400–700	$800–$1,700	$1,800+

What Else You'll Need

A good quality case, music stand and metronome are recommended for all instrumentalists. A sax player will also need a good neck strap or harness, reeds, a reed case, cork grease and a cleaning swab.

Reeds come in different grades according to strength. Higher numbers indicate stronger, harder reeds. Most beginners use softer reeds, such as a "2", and then move to stronger reeds, which produce a better tone, as they progress.

Sax Care and Maintenance

Tune the saxophone first when playing with other instruments by pulling the mouthpiece out or pushing it in to increase or decrease the length of the instrument.

Hold the saxophone by the bell. Be careful not to bend the keys or bump them out of alignment.

Assemble the instrument gently. Never force the parts together or put stress on the neck. If needed, rub a small amount of cork grease into the cork to allow the parts to slide together more easily.

After playing, take the instrument apart carefully. Remove the ligature and reed from the mouthpiece and store the reed in a case. Swab out the mouthpiece and then replace the ligature and cap. Drain any excess moisture out of the body. Then, while holding the keys closed, pull a cotton drop swab through the instrument to remove any remaining moisture inside. Don't leave the swab in the body.

Clean the outside of the instrument with a clean cotton cloth to remove fingerprints and oils.

Remove the neck strap and store the sax in the case. To prevent damage to the keys, don't keep extra items or music in the case. Be sure the instrument and case are dry before closing the case, since humidity can damage the pads.

Once a year or so, take the saxophone to a reputable repair shop for servicing. They will inspect, clean and oil the instrument, adjust keys and replace pads if needed.

Other Woodwind Instruments

Recorder

The recorder is also a popular first instrument, because it is small, light, simple and usually inexpensive. There are four sizes of recorders: Soprano, Alto, Tenor and Bass. Most beginners play the smallest one, the soprano recorder, which also has the highest sound. While good quality recorders are made from wood, most beginners start on very inexpensive plastic ones that cost $10-20. The player blows directly into the mouthpiece without a reed and covers the holes with different configurations of fingering to produce different pitches. Recorders are often used in group music classes. Most music written for recorder is early or Baroque music by composers such as Monteverdi, Lully, Charpentier, Purcell, Handel and Bach, however beginners often play folk tunes and other simple tunes that have been transcribed for the recorder.

Oboe

The oboe is used as the tuning instrument in orchestras because it has a stable pitch and stands out above the rest. While the oboe is a very important orchestral instrument, it is not often chosen by beginning musicians because it is harder to play than most of the other woodwinds. The oboe uses a double reed, which requires a different embouchure (position of the lips) and strong control. The player presses his or her lips together and turns them inward over the teeth before blowing in the reed. Oboe reeds are very delicate and players often make their own reeds. Oboists often start by playing clarinet first.

English Horn

Many oboists also play the English horn, a larger woodwind with a lower sound that uses the same fingering as the oboe.

Bassoon and Contrabassoon

Because they are large and heavy, bassoon and contrabassoon are often picked up later by woodwind players who started by playing flute or clarinet. Since playing them requires larger hands and a wider reach, players usually don't pick them up until age 12 or later. Both use a double reed. The bassoon has a deep, dark, rich, low tone. It consists of eight feet of wooden tubing that has been bent around. The player holds it to one side. The lower-sounding contrabassoon, which is made from 16 feet of wooden tubing, uses similar fingering.

BRASS

The Brass instrument family includes Cornet, Trumpet, Trombone, Baritone, Tuba and French Horn. The instruments in the Brass family are made of metal — often brass, but sometimes they are silver-plated or lacquered for easier care.

Brass players produce sound by blowing into their instruments while "buzzing" their lips to make the vibrations that create sound. Looser lips produce slower vibrations and, therefore, lower notes, while tighter lips produce quicker vibrations and higher notes. Playing brass instruments requires good breath and lip control.

Brass instruments are constructed of different lengths of long tubing that are bent and twisted around so that they can be held and carried. On each instrument, the pitch is changed by holding down different combinations of valves or shortening or lengthening a "slide" to adjust the length of the tubing. The differences in sound between the brass instruments is caused by differences in the shape, size and depth of the mouthpiece, the body shapes, and the length of the tubing.

Brass instruments are used in orchestras, concert bands, marching bands, jazz bands and brass ensembles. Orchestras typically include 1-2 each of trumpets, trombones, tubas and French horns.

Young musicians are often first drawn to brass instruments because they are shiny and loud! Most involve operating only three valves, so playing them requires less finger coordination than most other instruments. Maintenance is a little simpler than with woodwind or string instruments as well. Since the larger instruments require size and strength, beginners often pick up the trumpet, or even the smaller cornet, first. For those with long enough arms, trombone is also a popular first choice.

Trumpet

Beginning Trumpet
The trumpet is a popular beginning brass instrument because of its manageable size and musical versatility. Some trumpeters, particularly those who begin early, start first on the cornet, a smaller lighter instrument similar to the trumpet, on which it is a little easier to produce a good tone.

The trumpet player blows into the mouthpiece, while buzzing his or her lips, changing pitch and tone by changing the amount of air pressure, the shape of the lips and the combination of three valves pressed down to change the length of the tubing.

Playing trumpet requires breath and lip control and stamina, but less finger coordination than most other instruments. When kids get braces on their teeth, they need to adjust their embouchure (position of the lips) and technique and/or use some sort of device – a guard or cushion or pad or wax – to protect the lips from being cut by the braces.

Trumpet Music
Trumpets are used both as solo instruments and in orchestras, concert bands, marching bands, jazz bands and brass ensembles. With its high and loud voice, the trumpet often gets to play melody, in addition to providing harmony and rhythm. Trumpet players read music on the treble clef.

Opportunities For Trumpet Players

The trumpet is a transposing instrument. That is, music written for trumpet is transposed — raised or lowered to a different "key" — so that the note played sounds relatively higher or lower than the note written on the page. This practice allows trumpet players to use the same fingerings on different sizes of trumpets.

The standard trumpet is a "B-flat" trumpet. Advanced players may also play a "C" trumpet, a "piccolo" trumpet or other sizes of trumpets.

Shopping For a Trumpet

Pricing on trumpets varies according to workmanship and features. Most student trumpets are made with a two-piece bell (vs. a one-piece bell or seamless bell in more expensive models, which improves sound and projection).

Trumpets are made of brass, but come with different finishes. Most are lacquered or silver-plated. The more expensive silver-plate produces a slightly brighter tone.

> **Listening: Famous Trumpeters**
>
> **Classical:**
> ♪ Maurice André
> ♪ Adolph "Bud" Herseth
> ♪ Sergei Nakariakov
> ♪ Rafael Méndez
>
> **Jazz:**
> ♪ Louis Armstrong
> ♪ Miles Davis
> ♪ Dizzy Gillespie
> ♪ Wynton Marsalis
> ♪ Maynard Ferguson
> ♪ Clifford Brown
> ♪ Clark Terry
> ♪ Chet Baker
> ♪ Lee Morgan
> ♪ Roy Eldridge
> ♪ Arturo Sandoval
> ♪ Al Hirt
> ♪ Harry James
> ♪ Fats Navarro
> ♪ Doc Severinsen
> ♪ Chris Botti

The composition and fitting of valves is another factor that affects price. Student trumpets usually have durable nickel-plated valves, while more expensive trumpets are usually made with a corrosion-resistant alloy, Monel, or stainless steel.

A used trumpet may be a good value. If possible, have a teacher or an experienced trumpet player check any used instrument you are considering buying. Check to make sure the slides all operate smoothly and the water keys (also known as "spit valves") close tightly. Make sure the valves don't drag or stick. Check for dents, leaks or corrosion.

Sample Trumpet Prices

Beginner	Intermediate	Advanced
$300-500	$600-$900	$1,000-2,000

Listening: Famous Trumpet Music

- ♪ Haydn: Trumpet Concerto in E-flat Major
- ♪ Hummel: Trumpet Concerto in E-flat Major
- ♪ Mussorgsky: *Pictures at an Exhibition*
- ♪ Bach: *Brandenburg Concerto No. 2*
- ♪ Clarke: *Trumpet Voluntary*
- ♪ Mouret: *Rondeau* (*Masterpiece Theater* Theme)
- ♪ Beatles: *Penny Lane*
- ♪ Camarata: *Trumpeter's Prayer*
- ♪ Anderson: *Trumpeter's Lullaby*
- ♪ *Taps* and *Reveille* (usually played on a Bugle — a trumpet-like instrument that has no valves)

What Else You'll Need

A good case, music stand and metronome are recommended for all instrumentalists. Trumpet players will also need valve oil, slide grease and a mute.

Trumpet Care and Maintenance

After playing the trumpet, remove moisture inside by opening the water keys and blowing through it. Wipe off the outside with a clean soft cotton cloth to remove fingerprints and oils.

Valves usually need to be oiled every 2-3 days, or when needed, so they move up and down easily. Slides need to be greased about once a month. Some recommend cleaning the inside of your trumpet every 2-3 months, using a mouthpiece brush on the mouthpiece and a cleaning snake on the tubing and slides. Since this involves taking the instrument apart completely, others recommend (particularly for younger students) having it cleaned by a professional about once a year. Also take the trumpet to a professional if parts, such as the mouthpiece, caps or slides, become stuck. Don't try to force them apart.

Protect your trumpet by keeping it in its case. To avoid damage to slides and valves, don't keep anything other than small accessories in the case with it.

Trombone

Beginning Trombone

As with other brass instruments, the trombone player produces sound by buzzing his or her lips into a mouthpiece. Looser lips produce slower vibrations and, therefore, lower notes, while tighter lips produce quicker vibrations, and higher notes. Unlike other brass instruments that produce changes in pitch using valves, though, the trombone uses a slide, one tube fitted tightly over another, to adjust the length of the vibrating column of air. The trombone player pushes and pulls the slide in and out to one of seven different positions to create different pitches.

A trombone player needs a good sense of pitch to know exactly how far to push or pull the slide, along with a long enough right arm to control the slide. Trombone players often start around 4th or 5th grade in band programs.

Trombone Music

Trombones are played as solo instruments, in orchestras, bands, jazz groups and brass ensembles. The trombone plays in the mid-range between the higher trumpet and lower tuba. Because it uses a slide, it can make a unique "glissando" (continuous slide up or down between two notes) sound.

Trombone players read music on the bass clef.

Opportunities For Trombonists

Since trombone is not as popular a choice as some other instruments for beginners, there are usually good playing opportunities for trombonists.

Shopping For a Trombone

Some types of trombones have an optional "F" attachment that allows a player to use alternate slide positions when needed in difficult passages, but this is not usually needed for the first couple years of study.

Another option on trombones is the size of the "bore" — the inner diameter of the inner slide. The size of the bore affects the type of tone, with smaller bores producing a brighter tone and larger ones producing a broader tone. For a beginner, a trombone with a smaller bore is best, because it takes less air to produce an acceptable tone. More advanced players will play instruments with larger bores.

Listening: Famous Trombonists

Classical:
- ♪ Joseph Alessi
- ♪ Christian Lindberg

Jazz/Big Band:
- ♪ J.J. Johnson
- ♪ Jack Teagarden
- ♪ Frank Rosolino
- ♪ Arthur Pryor
- ♪ Bill Watrous
- ♪ Tommy Dorsey
- ♪ Glenn Miller

Most trombones have a lacquer finish, while some more expensive ones have plated finishes.

A used trombone may be a good option. If you are considering one, have an experienced player check it out for you. Make sure the slide moves freely and there are no large dents.

Sample Trombone Prices

Beginner	Intermediate	Advanced
$400–500	$600–$900	$1,000–2,000

Listening: Classical Pieces That Feature Trombone

♪ Ravel: *Bolero*
♪ Mozart: *Requiem*, "Tuba Mirum"
♪ Wagner: *Ride of the Valkyries*
♪ David: *Concertino for Trombone*
♪ Guilmant: *Morceau Symphonique*
♪ Rimsky-Korsakov: Trombone Concerto
♪ Mahler: Symphony No. 3
♪ Mozart: Concerto for Alto Trombone
♪ Mussorgsky: *Pictures At An Exhibition*, "Catacombs"
♪ *The Blue Bells of Scotland*

What Else You'll Need

A good case, music stand and metronome are recommended for all instrumentalists. Trombone players will also need slide cream for the hand slide, slide grease for the tuning slide, a mouthpiece brush, a cleaning snake and rod.

Trombone Care and Maintenance

Handle the trombone gently, being careful not to bump or dent the slide. Lock the slide when you are not playing.

Tune the trombone by adjusting the tuning slide. Pull it out to lower the pitch or push it in to raise the pitch.

As needed during your playing session and after playing, remove moisture inside the trombone by opening the water key (spit valve) and blowing through the instrument. Weekly, or as needed, wipe old slide cream off the inner slide and reapply a small amount of new cream. Carefully clean the insides of the outer slide with a cleaning rod wrapped in cheesecloth. Wipe off the outside with a soft cotton cloth to remove fingerprints and oils. Clean the mouthpiece with warm water and a mouthpiece brush.

Monthly, or as needed, lubricate the tuning slide with slide grease to keep it moving freely. Clean the inside of the trombone using lukewarm water, a little dish soap and a snake brush or cleaning rod.

Take the trombone to a professional if the mouthpiece or slides become stuck. Don't try to force anything together or apart.

Protect your trombone by keeping it in its case. To avoid damage to the slide and valves, don't keep books or anything but small accessories in the case with it.

French Horn

The French horn is a glorious instrument — and one of the most difficult to play well.

It consists of 12-13 feet of tubing that is coiled around, ending with a large "bell". The tubing is actually divided into two separate sets of tubing that are selected by a "thumb valve". One set of tubing is used for the higher notes and the other for the lower notes. The player operates this thumb valve and three other valves with the left hand, and places their right hand in the bell. Changes in pitch, tone and volume are produced by changing the configuration of valves that are pressed, the placement of the right hand in the bell, and the size of the embouchure (position of the lips and mouth). A French horn player, then, needs to have both a good sense of pitch and good coordination!

Listening: Famous French Horn Players

♪ Dennis Brain
♪ Barry Tuckwell
♪ Hermann Baumann
♪ Radek Baborak

Listening: Famous French Horn Pieces

♪ Wagner: "Horn Call", from *Siegfried*, Act II
♪ Mozart: Horn Concertos
♪ Strauss: Horn Concertos
♪ Saint-Saëns: *Morceau de Concert*
♪ Schumann: *Konzertstück* for 4 Horns and Orchestra, Op. 86
♪ Brahms: Horn Trio
♪ Beethoven: Horn Sonata

Besides being a solo instrument, the French horn is used in bands, orchestras, and chamber music. It can produce a large range of dynamics and tones and can serve in a variety of roles in an ensemble by playing either melody or harmony or by providing rhythm. In orchestras, French horn players sometimes specialize in either playing in the high range or low range.

Sample French Horn Prices

Beginner	Intermediate	Advanced
$800–1,200	$1,500–$2,500	$3,000+

Tuba

The tuba is the largest and lowest-sounding brass instrument.

The tuba isn't used much as a solo instrument, but it provides an important foundation or "oom-pah" role in orchestras and bands. In marching bands, a variation of the tuba, the Sousaphone, which wraps around the player so it can be carried, is used.

Because the tuba is so large, requires a lot of breath, and is relatively expensive, younger players usually start in band on a Baritone, which is similar to the tuba, but smaller and less expensive. Also, student tubas are available in 3/4 sizes.

Listening: Classical Music That Features Tuba

♪ Mussorgsky: *Pictures at an Exhibition*, "Bydlo"
♪ Vaughan Williams: Tuba Concerto

PERCUSSION

The Percussion family includes a variety of instruments that provide the pulse for music groups. Percussion players learn to play several instruments. Percussion instruments come in two varieties — those that are "pitched" and those that are "non-pitched".

"Pitched" percussion instruments include the Xylophone, Glockenspiel, Tubular Bells and the Timpani, a large drum that can produce different pitches as the skin (top) is tightened.

"Non-pitched" percussion instruments include the Bass Drum and the Snare Drum, as well as the Triangle, Cymbals, Gong, and Tambourine.

Beginning Drums and Percussion

Drums are made of skins stretched across a circular body or "shell", which is usually made of wood. When the skin is struck, it vibrates, causing the air inside the shell to vibrate. Drums with smaller bodies have a higher sound, while those with larger bodies create louder, deeper sounds. Drummers may use fingers or hands to strike the drums, or a variety of different types of sticks, such as wooden snare drumsticks, soft-headed bass drumsticks or wire brushes.

While percussionists learn to play several instruments, in school bands most start with the snare drum and a set of bells.

The snare drum has a set of wires strung across the bottom, which makes a rattling sound. It also has a snare switch, which can turn off the snares, so that the drum produces only a dull thud. In marching bands, snare drums are carried at the waist, while otherwise they are mounted on a stand. To keep the sound level down while they are learning the basics, beginning drummers use a "practice pad", a small pad that gives the feel of the snare drum.

The bells are a small version of the glockenspiel. Metal pieces of varying lengths are mounted on a wooden frame and struck with a mallet. The longer the length of the metal piece, the lower the sound. The pieces are arranged like a piano keyboard and usually have the note names indicated on each bar.

Drums in Music

Percussion plays an important role in most types of musical groups — orchestras, concert bands, marching bands, jazz bands, rock bands and in groups that play other types of pop and world music. Occasionally, drum players may "take a solo", but primarily they provide a vital rhythmic foundation.

Snare drums can provide a range of rhythms — from a basic pulse or "drum roll" to stylistic pop rhythm patterns.

Shopping For Drums: Percussion Sets for School Band

For school band, most beginning percussion students will need a set of bells, a practice pad, and a snare drum. Most school music groups will provide other percussion instruments, but some percussion players may eventually want their own sets. Check with the band director to see what is needed.

Shopping for Drums: Drum Sets

If learning drums to play jazz, rock or other popular music, a beginner can start with a bass drum, snare drum and ride or hi-hat cymbals. They will, however, eventually want a full set of four or five or more pieces. Buying the pieces in a package can offer a good value.

A 4-piece set can be adequate for jazz or rock. A 5-piece set adds another tom to expand the range. So a basic drum set includes:
- Bass Drum (with a foot pedal)
- Snare Drum (with a stand)
- 1-2 Tom-Toms (with mount)
- Floor Tom (with legs or stand)

Cymbals may be included in a set, but are often sold separately. A full set typically includes:
- Ride Cymbal (with stand)
- Crash Cymbal (with stand)
- 2 Hi-Hat Cymbals (with stand and clutch)

If you are buying a set, focus on the sound of the snare drum and hi-hat. Be sure to get all the hardware you will need. Usually, this will be included in a set.

Used drums can be a good option. If considering used drums, it's best to have an experienced drummer check them out for you. Be sure all the pieces are included. Check to be sure all the drums have both the top and bottom heads and all the tuning lugs in place. Look for the drums to be in good condition overall – the drumheads, exterior finish, and hardware.

Another option is to buy an electronic set with rubber or mesh pads. These can be used with headphones for practicing, a mixing board for recording or a sound system for performing. They can create a huge variety of sounds, which can be a lot of fun.

Also, it's fun to collect different types of rhythm instruments, including a variety that are used in folk, pop and world music.

What Else You'll Need

A music stand and metronome are recommended for all instrumentalists. Depending on how and where your drums will be played, cases may be a good investment. If you are playing a drum set, you will need a seat.

A drummer will also need a drum key (for tuning and adjusting drum heads) and drumsticks.

Drumsticks come in different types and sizes, which usually include a letter and a number. The letter indicates the type of music it is intended for — for example, "A" is for orchestral (or more acoustic) music, "B" for band, and "S" for "Street" music, such as marching band. The number indicates the circumference, with smaller numbers generally indicating greater circumference. Teachers often recommend "2B" size for beginners.

Drum Care and Maintenance

Because the drum shells are wooden, drums should be kept in a dry area out of direct sunlight. Avoid temperature extremes and if the drums have been in the cold, let them warm up gradually before playing. Keep drums and cymbals in cases when you are transporting them.

Drum heads may need to be replaced at some time. Follow the manufacturer's instructions regarding cleaning and supplies for your drums and cymbals.

VOICE

Singing is an excellent way to begin music. We all come already equipped with our instrument!

Beginning Singing
Any time is a good time to begin some form of singing. Some babies "sing" before they talk. Toddlers and preschoolers learn language, rhythm, coordination and more through songs and games that include music and movement. Kids naturally pick up songs they hear at home, through media, at school and church. Schools, churches and community groups often provide opportunities for young singers to join choirs and singing groups. Some schools also offer group voice classes that cover basic vocal technique. All of these are good ways to start. Those who aspire to be solo singers or top level choral or ensemble singers will at some point want to take private voice lessons.

Voice Lessons
When should one start voice lessons? Most private voice teachers prefer the student wait until at least age 12-14, as the voice simply needs time to develop physically. Younger aspiring singers can develop foundational musical skills before then through good quality choral programs and by learning to play piano or another instrument.

Boys' voices usually change gradually around age 12-13 as the larynx grows and vocal cords lengthen and thicken. As the voice gradually becomes lower and deeper, they may struggle a bit as they adjust to the new ranges.

Traditional voice teachers emphasize learning good vocal technique in order to prepare singers to be able to sing classical music. Besides working on songs in English, they often work with students on classic pieces in Italian, and possibly also German or French. Even for students who don't plan to sing opera or much other classical music, the technique learned with this type of teacher can be valuable.

Other teachers specialize in teaching "pop" or jazz techniques. Take caution to be sure these techniques don't injure the voice through strain or harsh vocal cord action.

Voice Lessons: The Basics

As in all forms of music, singers must learn to be good musicians — to be able to listen and reproduce pitches and tones accurately, to read music, and to blend appropriately with other singers.

Additionally, there are five main elements singers work on:

- ♪ **Breathing:** Breath is the foundation of singing. To produce good sound and develop vocal stamina, singers learn to breathe and control their breath using the diaphragm and abdominal muscles.
- ♪ **Relaxation:** To produce a free flowing sound, all tension must be released in the neck, throat and jaw areas.
- ♪ **Vowels:** Singing is a flow of vowels connected with consonants. Singers learn to form and adjust vowels to produce the best sound in different parts of their vocal range.
- ♪ **Resonance and Vocal Techniques:** Singers learn techniques that allow them to project their sound. They learn other techniques, such as "vibrato" or contemporary techniques, depending on the type of music they are singing and the "sound" they want to produce.

🎵 **Expression**: Singers work on developing their musicality and ability to "deliver" a song. This involves many elements, including conveying the meaning of the words, stage presence and gestures, musical and individual style, and timing.

Voice Teachers

Finding the right voice teacher can be a little trickier than finding other types of music teachers. Singing is simply more personal and the teaching of singing is more subjective, because vocal production isn't visible. A teacher can't physically adjust the student's vocal production, but instead has to work through techniques such as modeling, explanation, examples, imagery and experimentation.

When looking for a voice teacher, along with the general considerations for finding a music teacher, consider particularly the following:

🎵 **Training**: What training have they had in vocal pedagogy — that is, teaching voice? It is one thing to have a good voice and to sing well oneself, but understanding vocal production and being able to teach vocal technique is a separate and crucial element.

🎵 **Style and Repertoire**: What style of singing do they teach? Which type of music do they know best?

🎵 **Communication and Fit**: Because vocal technique is intangible and singing style is more individual, it's particularly important to have a good teacher-student fit.

🎵 **Results**: If you can, listen to several of the teacher's students. There is often a "sound" the teacher works toward. Do you like that "sound"? Watch out for danger signs, such as tension or vocal damage from too much harsh use of the vocal cords.

FOLK INSTRUMENTS

Beyond Guitar

Beginning folk musicians often pick up a guitar first. There are several other good instrument choices for beginners, though. Learning to play a folk instrument can be a relatively easy way to enjoy making music either by oneself or with others. Singers also enjoy being able to accompany themselves with folk instruments' different sounds and techniques.

Here, we'll briefly cover a few favorite folk instruments for beginners – autoharp, dulcimer, banjo and harmonica.

Autoharp

The autoharp is probably the easiest instrument to pick up to provide simple accompaniment for folk songs.

To play chords to accompany singing, all one has to do is press down on the buttons with the desired chord names and strum. Depressing a chord button lowers a chord bar that automatically dampens all the strings not included in the chord. You can't go wrong.

Children and beginning autoharp players often place the instrument in their lap or on a table in front of them. Some use their right hand to select the buttons and their left hand to strum, while others prefer playing the buttons with the left hand and crossing their right hand over to strum. More advanced players may "hug" the autoharp, holding it upright against their left shoulder, using their left hand to work the buttons and their right hand to strum. (Since they can't see the chord button labels this way, they have to develop a "feel" for their locations, but this position allows them to play standing up and to move.)

Beginners can simply strum chords using their fingers or picks. As they progress, they can play more complicated strumming patterns. Besides strumming chord patterns, more advanced players also pick out melody notes, enabling them to not only accompany singing, but to play solos in a variety of styles.

Standard autoharps come in two sizes, 15 Chord, which allows the player to play standard folk chords in 7 keys (C, G, D, A, E, F, Bb) and 21 Chord, which expands the number of possible keys to 11. In addition to the instrument itself, an autoharp player will want a variety of thumb and fingerpicks, a tuner and a tuning wrench.

As with other stringed instruments, the autoharp should be kept in a good case away from extreme temperatures and direct sunlight. If it has been in the cold, it should be allowed to warm up in the case before playing.

Clean the autoharp by wiping the strings with a damp cloth. To remove dust underneath the strings, wrap a cloth around a ruler and carefully push it under the strings.

> **Listening: Autoharp Players & Styles**
> ♬ Maybelle Carter
> ♬ Kilby Snow
> ♬ Michael Stanwood
> ♬ Brian Bowers
> ♬ PJ Harvey
> ♬ Patrick Couton

Change strings when they break or sound dull. At some point, the felt on the chord bars may need to be replaced as well.

Mountain Dulcimer

The mountain dulcimer is another fairly easy instrument for beginners. It has a long narrow wooden body with a fretted fingerboard and usually three or four strings.

> **Listening: Famous Dulcimer Players**
> ♪ Jean Ritchie
> ♪ Richard Farina
> ♪ Don Pedi
> ♪ Stephen Seifert
> ♪ David Schnaufer

The player places the dulcimer in their lap or on their knees. With the right hand, they use a pick, a quill or their fingers to strum or pick the strings. With the left hand, they press down on the strings either with their fingers or with a "noter", a small stick, to sound different pitches and form chords. Experienced dulcimer players use a variety of tunings. For the most-used tuning for beginners, Ionian (Major) tuning, the melody string, the one closest to the player (or the two melody strings on a four-string dulcimer), and the middle string are tuned in unison. The bass note is then tuned a perfect fifth lower. This produces the traditional sound of a melody with a drone accompaniment.

Dulcimer players can play as soloists, accompany singing, or play with other folk instruments. Music for dulcimer is often written out in tablature, a type of diagram showing which strings to play and which fret positions to use.

As with other stringed instruments, the dulcimer should be kept in a good case away from extreme temperatures. The strings should be wiped gently after playing and changed as needed. Special dulcimer string sets are available, but some players use banjo strings.

Note: Another instrument referred to as a dulcimer is the hammered dulcimer, a trapezoid-shaped instrument with many strings played by hitting individual strings with light "hammers". It's a beautiful instrument, but much more expensive and complicated to learn than the mountain dulcimer.

Banjo

The forerunner of the banjo was brought to America from Africa by slaves. In the early 19th century, it evolved from a simple 3-stringed instrument to the 5-stringed instrument we know today. Over time, its popularity has varied considerably. For instance, after becoming very popular in America during the 19th century, it practically died out by 1940.

The banjo has a very happy sound. While people usually think of it first as a bluegrass instrument, over the years the banjo has been used to play ragtime, gospel, classical arrangements and even jazz and pop music. It's played in bluegrass bands, Dixieland bands, by itself and as an accompanying instrument.

The most popular type of banjo today has five strings, with the fifth one running only halfway down the neck. (Four-stringed tenor and plectrum banjos used in traditional and Dixieland jazz, don't have the short string and are tuned differently.) Like a guitar, the banjo has "frets", slightly raised metal bars that go across the neck, that indicate where to place your fingers to play each note. As with guitar, different pitches are produced by pressing down on the strings at different points on the neck. In standard tuning ("G tuning"), the short fifth string is tuned to high G, with the other four strings being tuned from low to high (top to bottom as the banjo is held in playing position) as D, G, B, and D.

Listening: Banjo Players & Styles
- ♪ Earl Scruggs
- ♪ Béla Fleck
- ♪ Tony Trischka
- ♪ Pete Seeger
- ♪ Fred Van Eps (ragtime)
- ♪ Ralph Stanley (gospel)
- ♪ Noam Pickelny
- ♪ Jens Kruger
- ♪ Alison Brown

Banjo players may play by ear, play chord patterns from lead sheets, or play precise arrangements written out in tablature that indicates rhythm, which string to play, and where to fret it. They learn strumming, picking and left-hand techniques similar to guitar techniques, as well as picking techniques unique to banjo.

There are two types of 5-string banjos — the louder, brighter-sounding wood-backed Resonator banjo used in bluegrass and the lighter old-time style Open-back banjo. Besides the instrument itself, most banjo players will also need a good case, a banjo strap, extra strings, a thumb pick, fingerpicks, a capo to allow for playing in different keys and some sort of mute (either a purchased banjo mute that fits on top of the bridge or a cloth of some sort to stuff inside the back).

Harmonica

A harmonica can provide a fun and inexpensive means of making music.

Harmonicas come in a variety of sizes. There are two basic types — diatonic and chromatic. Standard diatonic harmonicas have 10 holes and can play 19 notes in a specific key. Chromatic harmonicas have 12 holes and can play a full 12-note scale. Here, we'll cover the diatonic type harmonica more frequently used by beginners, folk and blues players.

Inside the harmonica case, reeds vibrate when air moves across them. A harmonica player produces different tones by either blowing air into or drawing air out of specific holes. To play just one note, the player blocks the other holes with their lips or tongue. On a diatonic harmonica, they can also produce a chord by blowing across any three adjacent holes at once.

Typically, a beginner would start with a "C" harmonica. On this instrument, blowing into any three adjacent holes will produce a "C" chord using some combination of the notes C, E and G. The holes in the middle (position 4-7) can be used to play a full "C" scale (C, D, E, F, G, A, B). For instance, blowing into hole number 4 produces a "C", while drawing air out produces a "D". Other common chords used in folk music and blues, the subdominant ("F" in the key of C) and dominant ("G" in the key of C) chords can be played by drawing air out of other combinations of holes.

Because a diatonic harmonica only plays in one key, a more advanced player who wants to play with others will usually acquire a collection of harmonicas. For example, a blues player might have a kit that includes C, A, D, E, G, F and Bb harmonicas. Traditionally, harmonicas have been most used in blues and folk music, but they are also used today in jazz, rock, country and other music genres.

Harmonica players often play by ear, but sometimes music is written out for them in tablature that indicates the hole numbers to play and whether to blow in or draw out air. They learn to produce different effects using their hands, tongue and breath.

Listening: Harmonica Players & Styles
- ♪ Larry Adler
- ♪ Little Walter
- ♪ Charlie McCoy
- ♪ The Harmonicats
- ♪ Stevie Wonder
- ♪ Howard Levy
- ♪ Toots Thielemans
- ♪ Sonny Boy (John Lee) Williamson I
- ♪ Sonny Terry

While very cheap harmonicas are available, trying to learn on one can be frustrating, so it's best to buy a good brand harmonica, such as Hohner, Lee Oskar, Suzuki, Hering or Seydel. (Buying a used harmonica or sharing one is not recommended.)

To care for a harmonica, keep it clean. Don't eat or drink anything other than water while practicing and playing.

Other Folk Instruments

Folk musicians often play several different instruments. Singers may learn and use several different folk instruments to add variety to their accompaniments. Simple wind instruments, such as a tin whistle, or simple rhythm instruments can easily add color and energy to musical arrangements.

It's fun to play with different combinations of instruments and it's usually relatively easy for players with experience on one folk instrument to pick up another. For instance, the fiddle (violin) and the mandolin both use the same string arrangement – G, D, A and E. While most stringed folk instruments do use different chord fingerings, folk harmonies are usually relatively simple, so players may only need to know a few chords. Each instrument has its unique differences, however many techniques transfer easily to from one stringed instrument to another. For example, the same type of right-hand "hammer on" and "pull off" techniques are used by bluegrass guitar, banjo and mandolin players.

SHOPPING FOR MUSICAL INSTRUMENTS

Buying a Musical Instrument: The Basics

These days musical instrument buyers have many options. Instruments for beginners can be found at both local or online stores that specialize in particular types of musical instruments or at larger retail or online stores that carry a broad range of musical and electronic gear.

When deciding where to go for an instrument, there are four major factors to consider:

- ♪ Buying From Specialty Stores vs. "Big Box" Stores
- ♪ Buying Online vs. In Person
- ♪ Renting vs. Buying
- ♪ Buying New vs. Used

Specialty Music Stores vs. "Big Box" Stores

Stores that specialize in specific types of instruments (for example, a violin shop or a guitar store) typically offer a broad range of their specialty instruments — for example, several brands and a full price range. Specialty music stores often have very knowledgeable and experienced staff that can advise buyers during the buying process. Some specialty stores will even allow potential higher-level buyers to take instruments out "on approval" so they can play them for longer periods of time before making a final commitment.

If you are buying your instrument from a specialty music store, inquire about a trade-in policy. When the student is ready for a larger or higher quality instrument, they will often give back a good portion of the original instrument price for a trade-in.

Large "big box" stores that offer a broad range of music and electronic gear (or even general merchandise) may offer good deals, especially on "outfits" for beginners, as well as offering a range of other accessories and equipment that can be useful and fun. Be cautious when considering buying very inexpensive instruments, though. Some are poorly constructed and apt to frustrate beginning students. It's usually best to invest a little more and to stick with established brands.

Buying Musical Instruments Online vs. In Person

Many people are most comfortable buying an instrument in person. At local stores, the buyer can usually try out a range of instruments and judge the tone, feel and appearance. Local stores often also have access to skilled experts who can help with maintenance and repair.

Online stores can give the buyer access to a broad variety and range of instruments no matter where they live. Also, prices are often attractive. Here are some suggestions if you are buying online:

- ♪ **Resources:** Online stores often have videos and other help resources via website or phone to help you make the best selection. Use these resources to help make decisions about sizes, brands, accessories and other choices. Also, your local music teacher can likely provide useful advice.
- ♪ **Shipping:** Be sure to consider shipping costs and methods in your purchase decision. Instruments should be well-protected and insured for damage during shipping.
- ♪ **Returns:** Check out the return policy before you buy. It is reasonable to want to try the instrument and check out the quality and sound before being fully committed.

- **Reviews:** As with anything you buy online, it's wise to check the seller's reputation.

Buying vs. Renting a Musical Instrument

Stores that sell musical instruments often offer rental options, including rent-to-buy options. The monthly instrument rental fee often also includes insurance against damage. Renting an instrument can be a good option for a beginner. General benefits of renting vs. buying include these:
- Renting gives beginners a chance to try a certain instrument without making a big investment.
- Renting allows a student to try out different brands and specific instruments before committing to a certain one.
- Renting allows you to make your investment over time instead of in one large payment.
- For instruments that are available in smaller sizes, renting can be a good option, because the student will "move up" into larger sizes as they grow.

Benefits of buying instead of renting include:
- Buying gives you some "equity" to build on. You can later recover some of your investment when you sell or trade in the instrument. Stores that specialize in musical instrument sales often have a trade-in policy that gives you some credit towards an upgrade or larger-sized instrument when you turn in the one originally bought from them.
- Buying can be a better financial deal over time, so it often makes sense when the student has a good level of commitment or when siblings may use the instrument in the future.

Buying Used Instruments

If you know what to look for, a used instrument can be a good deal, as well as a way to acquire rare instruments. Most beginning instrument buyers, and even many more experienced ones, don't have the expertise to judge the value and condition of instruments well, though. In that case, ask for guidance from your music teacher or a knowledgeable friend. In the case of more expensive instruments, it may be worth hiring a professional to assist in the purchase — for instance, hiring a piano technician to check out a used piano or obtaining an appraisal on an expensive stringed instrument.

What Else You'll Need

Besides the instrument itself, a few accessories will be needed. Some of this is specific to the type of instrument. For instance, a violinist will need a bow, extra strings and rosin. A clarinetist will need reeds. A brass player will need valve oil. A tuner is recommended for string players.

Most musicians will need a good case to transport their instrument (acoustic pianists, organists and singers excepted!), as well as a music stand. A metronome is recommended for all musicians

LEARNING PARTNERS

SEVEN MODES OF MUSICAL LEARNING

Learning to produce sound from an instrument is just one part of becoming a good musician. An effective music learning program will include many elements:

Listening: Music, after all, is meant to be heard. Musicians learn to listen at several different levels. They listen for melody, harmony, rhythm, dynamics and tone. They listen for patterns and form. They listen for how parts fit together. They listen for technical precision and for overall feeling. They learn to make distinctions between different sounds, tones, pitches and rhythms. By listening well, they learn to match pitches, to blend with other instruments, and to repeat back rhythms and phrases.

Musicians also learn to play more musically by listening to very skilled musicians. They can also accelerate their learning of pieces by listening frequently to good recordings.

Music Theory & Principles: Musicians become more skilled by understanding the underlying principles of how music works. They learn and practice musical vocabulary and shortcuts, such as chords and scales, that help them learn to play and memorize pieces more quickly.

Music Reading: Good musicians are able to read printed musical symbols and play them accurately. As they practice this skill, they're able to read more difficult music faster and with more accuracy.

Technique: Musicians are always working on being able to produce good tone and to play rapidly and evenly. To do this, they use exercises especially designed to improve strength, flexibility, speed and tone. They also learn ways to make different kinds of sounds and effects — like we might speak using different tones of voice or punctuation.

Repertoire: Musicians continually add to and improve the collection of pieces they play. On new pieces, they work first on playing accurately. Then they "polish" the piece to make it more musical. Lastly, they memorize it and review it to keep it in "playing condition".

Style: Musicians learn ways to play different types of music as their composers would have intended. They may also develop their own style — favorite unique ways of playing and sounding.

Performing: One of the best ways to progress as a musician is to perform often for others. Getting ready to perform requires good practice. Learning to perform involves not only learning to play music accurately and musically, but also learning to connect with an audience.

LEARNING OPTIONS

Beginning musicians usually start to learn to play their instrument in one of three ways:
- ♪ Working with a private teacher
- ♪ Taking a class or joining a musical group
- ♪ "Teaching themselves" using independent learning resources

What's the best way? It depends. Generally, a student makes the fastest and best progress with private instruction, but other methods may also work well in certain situations. To determine what might work well in your own situation, consider these factors:
- ♪ *What options are available in your area?*
- ♪ *How do you learn best?*
- ♪ *What are your goals?*
- ♪ *What's your budget?*

Let's explore the benefits and issues with each major learning option.

Working With a Private Teacher
Benefits:
- ♪ Working with a private teacher provides flexibility. The teacher is able to address your goals and interests, give you personal attention, tailor his or her teaching to how you learn best, and adjust to your learning speed.

- ♪ The teacher is able to watch and listen to you closely and give you specific, individualized feedback. Because of this, the student is more likely to develop good playing technique.
- ♪ Most people find that working with a private music teacher provides built-in motivation to practice, since they know that they will have to face the teacher and play their assigned exercises and pieces at a certain time.

Issues:
- ♪ It's important to find a teacher who is not only musically qualified, but is a good fit for you, your goals and interests. (The next chapter will cover this in depth.)
- ♪ You'll need to work into the teacher's schedule.
- ♪ Private lessons generally involve a bigger investment than other methods.

Other:
- ♪ Some private teachers also hold group lessons for their students, in which they cover general topics, conduct exercises, reinforce learning and encourage performance.
- ♪ Students taking private lessons often also join groups for playing and performance opportunities.

Taking a Class or Joining a Musical Group

Beginners often start by taking a group music class, such as a guitar class or piano class or by joining a school music group, such as band or orchestra.

Benefits:
- ♪ Learning in a group setting can be fun. There's usually less pressure. The students often develop camaraderie.
- ♪ Fees for group learning are usually quite a bit less than private lesson fees.

Issues:
- ♪ Students need to fit into the group schedule.
- ♪ Students need to adjust to the pace of the group.

♪ Students receive less individualized attention than they would get with private instruction. If the student aspires to higher levels of playing, it's important to make sure they are developing technique that will serve them well as they advance.

Other:
- ♪ There's usually some sort of built-in progression from one class to the next or from one performance level to the next.
- ♪ Group learning and performance can be combined effectively with private lessons.

Using Independent Learning Resources

Benefits:
- ♪ Learning can take place at the student's convenience.
- ♪ Materials are available to anyone anywhere.
- ♪ Students can move at their own pace.
- ♪ Students can seek out materials that fit with their specific musical interests.
- ♪ Learning using online or packaged learning materials can be very cost-effective.

Issues:
- ♪ This type of learning requires a high level of self-motivation.
- ♪ Some beginners prefer a more personal touch.
- ♪ There's less flexibility within the teaching method.
- ♪ If feedback is available, it is less individualized.

Other:
- ♪ Self-instruction or self-paced instruction can work very well for a student who already has a musical background.
- ♪ A student using this type of learning method can increase motivation and accountability by banding together with a local "buddy". It also works well to supplement this type of learning with group performance opportunities.

HOW TO CHOOSE A PRIVATE MUSIC TEACHER

Finding a teacher who is a good fit for you and your musical purpose will make all the difference. Before you set out to find a teacher, ask yourself these questions:

- ♪ What do you hope to achieve by taking lessons?
- ♪ How much time are you willing and able to devote to practicing?
- ♪ How far are you willing to travel? What times would you be available on a regular basis for lessons?

Then, when you look at your choices of teachers, consider these factors:

Music Style
Find out which style or styles of music the teacher prefers and teaches. If they don't specify something else, most teachers teach "classical" music. That is, they teach students to read music and prepare them to play pieces by classical masters such as Bach, Mozart, and Beethoven. Some teachers specify that they teach jazz or "pop" styles. While some teachers can cover a range of styles, most have a preferred style.

Type and Level of Student

Find out which types of students the teacher prefers to teach. Some teachers specialize in teaching younger children and beginners, while others work only with students who already play at a certain skill level. Some want to work only with "serious" musicians and will expect a high level of commitment, while others are happy to work with families hoping to enrich their lives through music. Many welcome adults.

Methodology

Teachers have a variety of approaches to the following elements involved in teaching music:
- ♪ Reading music
- ♪ Technique
- ♪ Selecting and learning pieces
- ♪ Musicianship
- ♪ Performing

Ask about their methodology and which books or software they will use in teaching.

Musical and Teaching Background

While public school music teachers usually hold a college degree in Music Education (or a degree in Music with a teaching certificate), there are no specific educational requirements for private music teachers, so they come from a wide range of backgrounds. Background will be one of several important factors to consider in finding the right teacher for your situation. Depending on your age, stage and goals, other factors, such as ability to build a rapport and motivate a student, or practical matters, such as location and fees, may be equally important. In evaluating potential teachers' backgrounds, consider three factors:
- ♪ **Academic background:** You can expect a teacher with a college degree in music to be qualified in several ways. Colleges, universities and conservatories offer a few different types of

degrees in music. Most focus largely on classical music, however some programs include jazz and other types of music as well.

- Bachelor of Music: A Bachelor of Music degree requires intensive music study, usually including music theory, music history and solo and ensemble performance. B.M. candidates often specialize in areas such as Applied Music (performance), Pedagogy (teaching) or Composition. If a teacher has earned a B.M. degree, it's likely that they have a good understanding of classical music and a good range of repertoire on their main instrument.
- Bachelor of Music Education: A Bachelor of Music Education degree also requires intensive music study, along with courses that prepare the candidate to teach in public schools. B.M.E. students usually choose to specialize in instrumental or vocal music, preparing to teach general music courses and/or conduct school orchestras, bands or choirs. They typically have familiarity with a wider range of instruments, as well as a high level of skill on at least one.
- Bachelor of Arts in Music: Candidates for a Bachelor of Arts degree in Music also are typically required to take a number of courses in music theory, music history and performance, along with a range of liberal arts courses.

♪ **Practical music background:** What is the teacher's experience as a musician? How well do they play themselves? What type of music have they played? What performance experience have they had? In music performance careers, what really matters is what you can do. Not all professional musicians have a degree in music or a degree at all.

♪ **Teaching background:** What training or experience have they had in teaching itself? Are they certified to teach certain methods, such as the Suzuki Method?

Expectations

You'll want to get a feel for what a teacher will be expecting of students (and parents). For example, what are their expectations for music practice? Do they expect students to participate in group classes in addition to private lessons? Do they expect participation in solo recitals or group performances?

Fees

Of course, you'll need to find out about fees. Teachers consider several factors when they determine their fees, including:
- ♪ Their background, qualifications and experience
- ♪ The frequency and length of the lessons
- ♪ The location of the lesson
- ♪ The "going rate" among music teachers in their area

You'll also need to be aware of the teacher's policies regarding payment, cancellations and other practical matters. For instance, teachers may expect payment upfront by the month or even for a semester. Teachers usually also specify policies for notice required to reschedule or cancel a lesson.

Location

Teachers may teach lessons in one location or several. Many teach in home studios, while others teach in schools, stores, churches or community centers. Some will even come to your home, usually for a slightly higher fee to cover their transportation costs.

How To Find A Music Teacher

There are several ways you can go about locating potential music teachers.
- ♪ **Word of Mouth:** Often students connect with teachers after hearing about a friend's experience. This can be a very good method, especially if you and the friend have similar interests and goals.

- ♪ **Schools and Music Organizations:** School music teachers and local performing arts organizations often maintain lists of local music teachers. Nearby colleges or universities may have faculty or students who are available to teach students in the community.
- ♪ **Credentialing Organizations:** Organizations that grant credentials to teachers of their method (for example, The Suzuki Method) often maintain lists of teachers who have completed their training.
- ♪ **Retail Music Stores and Schools:** Stores that sell musical instruments and equipment often also have teaching space or can provide referrals to local teachers.
- ♪ **Online Sources:** An online search of music teachers for your area will likely turn up some resources as well, including both individual teachers and referral networks.

Interviewing Potential Music Teachers: What To Ask

Here are some questions to ask teachers you are considering:
- ♪ *What types of students do you work with best?*
- ♪ *Tell me about your methodology.*
- ♪ *What is your musical and teaching background?*
- ♪ *What are your expectations of your students?*
- ♪ *What are your expectations of your students' parents? How do you communicate with parents?*
- ♪ *What is your availability?*
- ♪ *What are your fees?*

One of the big factors in successful music teacher/student relationships is simply rapport. Does the student like the teacher? Do they "get" each other? Is there the right type of structure and/or flexibility for the student? Is the teacher responsive to the student's needs? Does he or she give the student the right amount and type of direction and support? How does the student feel after the lesson — relieved or inspired?

If possible, talk with current or former students about their experience. Listen to how they play or sing and how they talk about their learning experience.

Another way to get a feel for whether a teacher is a good fit is by attending a performance of their students or observing a class or lesson.

Some teachers will ask you to come for an audition appointment or trial lesson. This is an opportunity for both the teacher and student to see if they're a good fit. It's customary to pay for this type of appointment.

Caution: Most people promoting themselves as music teachers are wonderful, qualified professionals who love young people and love teaching. But there are always stories you hear about kids who ended up hating music lessons because they had a "bad" teacher. (It could have actually been that the student wasn't very interested in or committed to their music lessons to begin with!) In some cases, this simply meant they didn't have a teacher who was a good fit for them or with their goals. Or perhaps the teacher was either not a good musician or not good at teaching (or both). Occasionally, it turns out that they studied with a teacher who didn't love teaching. Perhaps the teacher really wanted to be performing, but had to "fall back on" teaching to earn a living. (Note: Some performers are also wonderful teachers.) Perhaps they just didn't like working with young children. One thing is certain: *The enthusiasm a teacher has for music and for teaching is bound to be contagious. And the love they have for their students will be felt. Don't overlook those factors.*

Working With A Music Teacher

Selecting a qualified music teacher who is a good fit for the student is a big step. You can also increase the impact of lessons by working with the teacher to support and multiply their efforts.

Teaching and Learning Success

A successful teacher will:

- ♪ **Guide the student toward self-sufficiency.** The successful teacher will guide their students to eventually be able to play well without them. They will make sure their students understand musical principles. They will work to be sure they can read music well and play accurately. They will help students recognize when they are using good technique and playing musically. Most will hope to inspire the student to love playing, to love listening and to love sharing music.
- ♪ **Stretch, but not stress.** The successful teacher will understand the student and know just the right amount to push them to achieve progress without causing undue stress or frustration.
- ♪ **Inspire.** An indicator of the teacher's success is how the student feels both before and after their lesson. Do they look forward to the lesson or dread it? (Note: Sometimes students feel a little of both — often because they did not practice very much.) Do they walk away feeling at least a small sense of success, progress, hope and inspiration?

What Works For Teachers

A teacher will appreciate:

- ♪ **Your commitment to music learning.** Teachers love to work with students who embrace musical goals and commit to active participation in lessons and practice.
- ♪ **Your professional respect.** Most music teachers have invested a great deal in preparing to be able to do their work. While most also enjoy teaching music, just as other types of professionals, they do rely on it for their living. They reserve your lesson time for you, so it is important that you show up regularly and promptly and compensate them appropriately. For example, unless there is an extreme emergency, if you don't show up for a lesson without giving reasonable notice and rescheduling, it is appropriate to pay them for the time they reserved for you.

- ♪ **Your participation in events.** Offer to pass out programs, take photos or provide snacks for student performances and events.
- ♪ **Your referrals.** Most new students come to teachers through referrals from other students and their families. If you have had a good experience, spread the word. Most teachers will be very happy to talk with your friends. Let them know of that possibility, so they will be prepared for an inquiry about lessons.
- ♪ **Your kind words.**

Communication & Involvement

Good communication with your teacher is important. Be sure to read any information the teacher provides, such as policy and scheduling information, newsletters, tips or suggestions.

Some teachers welcome parents to sit in on lessons. If this is an option for you, take the opportunity to quietly observe the lesson and learn about the teacher's approach. Learn what to pay attention to during practice.

Do ask questions. Most teachers will welcome this. Find a good time to ask questions. The best time to ask is usually during your lesson time. If you need to ask at a different time, check to see what works best for the teacher. Most have tight schedules, so, even if they'd like to, it's hard for them to take extra time after a student's lesson or during their teaching day. Many also have other obligations, including performances and family responsibilities. So find out how they prefer to communicate — e.g. by email, by phone — and when the best time is to contact them.

THE SUZUKI METHOD

The Suzuki Method is a method of music instruction developed by Japanese violinist Shinichi Suzuki. While the method was originally developed for violin students, materials are now also available for viola, cello, bass, piano, flute, harp, classical guitar, recorder, voice, organ and trumpet.

Suzuki Philosophy

Much of the difference between the Suzuki Method and other methods of musical instruction is a result of the underlying philosophy.

Talent Education: Dr. Suzuki believed that musical ability can be developed in all children. According to Dr. Suzuki, "Musical ability is not an inborn talent but an ability which can be developed. Any child who is properly trained can develop musical ability, just as all children develop the ability to speak their mother tongue. The potential of every child is unlimited."

"Mother-Tongue Approach": Dr. Suzuki recognized that all children naturally learn to speak their native language through listening, imitation and encouragement. He applied this concept to music education, calling his method the "mother-tongue approach."

Character Education: The goal of Suzuki education is not only to develop musicianship, but to develop character through the study of music.

"The main concern for parents should be to bring up their children as noble human beings. That is sufficient. If this is not their greatest hope, in the end the child may take a road contrary to their expectations. Children can play very well. We must try to make them splendid in mind and heart also."

– Shinichi Suzuki

Suzuki Music Method: Characteristics

There are several characteristics that differentiate the Suzuki Method from other methods of music instruction:

Beginning Early
While it is never too late to begin, Suzuki students often start as early as age three or four.

Listening
Listening is a vital part of the Suzuki method. Students are encouraged to listen to their pieces every day.

Parental Involvement
Parents of early Suzuki students participate in lessons with their child and learn how to support the child in practice sessions between lessons.

Group Learning and Performance

Along with their own private lessons, Suzuki students take part in group lessons. They play often with and for each other in low-key performances, so that performing is very natural to them.

Delayed Music Reading

Just as children learn to talk well before they learn to read, Suzuki students concentrate first on learning basic technique and musical skills through listening and imitation, and then later learn to read music.

Technique Developed Through Repertoire

Rather than working on separate technical exercises, Suzuki students gradually build technique through technical problems presented within the context of musical pieces they learn.

Review

After learning a piece, Suzuki students keep it in their repertoire by reviewing it regularly.

INDEPENDENT LEARNING PROGRAMS

Online and packaged music learning programs provide an alternative to working with a private teacher in person or participating in a group class.

This type of independent learning can work well for many people. Some of the benefits of this type of learning are:

- ♪ Access: No matter where you live, online or packaged music learning programs can give you access to a variety of teachers, methods and styles.
- ♪ Flexibility: While some online teachers do schedule time-specific sessions, most programs of this type make lessons with audio or video recordings and other materials available to use at your convenience.
- ♪ Cost: Costs vary greatly, but, because they don't require one-on-one real-time teacher presence, these programs can often be relatively inexpensive.

This type of learning is not for everyone, though. Here are some of the challenges:

- ♪ Discipline: This type of learning requires discipline. When you sign up for one of these programs, you've paid, whether you use it or not. They are usually a good value overall, but only if you use them!

- ♪ Feedback: With this type of program, any feedback the student receives is more limited in scope than with private lessons, where a teacher can directly address technique and musicality issues, as well as accuracy of pitch, rhythm and tone.
- ♪ Practice Motivation: Almost every music student practices more the day or two before their lesson than the rest of the week. Having to actually face a teacher can provide motivation to practice. It's easier to procrastinate with a less personal "teacher".

Here are some ways to find good programs:
- ♪ Referrals: A recommendation from a like-minded friend who has used the program is ideal.
- ♪ Sample: Some programs will provide a free sample lesson to try.
- ♪ Reviews: Program reviews may be available online, in newsletters or other periodicals. If you can find a reputable review source, these often provide helpful detail and perspective from users.

If you choose this type of learning option, here are some tips to make it work:
- ♪ Select a program that's a good fit for you.
- ♪ Schedule a regular "lesson time", as well as regular practice times.
- ♪ Find a learning "buddy" – someone who is using the same or a similar program. Challenge each other to keep up practicing.
- ♪ Schedule a performance. You are more likely to practice regularly and effectively if you know you are going to have to show up and play in front of an audience, even if it's a small, friendly one.

PERFORMANCE GROUPS

Playing in a musical group can be a wonderful way to both enjoy music and develop musicianship and skill.

Here are some factors to consider when investigating opportunities with performance groups:

Type of Group: *Is it a fit?*
Find out what kind of music the group performs and check out who belongs. Attend a performance if possible. Do you like the music? What's the musical background of a typical member? Can you see yourself in the group, either now or in the future? It's good to have a little challenge – either too much or too little could be frustrating.

The Organization: *Who's behind it and what's the purpose?*
Find out about the organization itself. Many groups, of course, are affiliated with public or private schools. Other groups are affiliated with private music studios or schools, colleges or universities, or other arts organizations. Some are stand-alone community groups run by a board comprised of members, parents or friends. Differences may show up in a group's philosophy, funding, leadership and policies due to the influence of the backing organization.

Membership: *How do I join? Is an audition required?*
Some established musical performing groups are open to anyone who would like to join, regardless of skill level or experience. Others will require an audition, a "try out", where a conductor will listen to potential members play or sing and decide which ones to bring in depending on the needs and skill level of the group. Some performance organizations have multiple groups, so an audition is needed to decide which group is the best fit for the musician at the current time. (Note: Some groups with open membership also require auditions, but these are just for placement — to decide which section is the best fit or to assign "chairs".)

If an audition is required, find out when auditions are held and what is expected at the audition. Audition requirements generally increase along with the expected level of play. For instance, a regional youth orchestra audition will usually require a string player to play scales, two contrasting pieces and a sight-reading piece — excerpts from an orchestral piece the player will see for the first time at the audition. A middle-school choral director, on the other hand, might just ask a singer to sing a familiar piece, such as "My Country 'Tis of Thee", in order to decide whether the singer should sing in the 1st Soprano, 2nd Soprano or Alto section.

Progression: *What's the future?*
Music organizations often have more than one group to accommodate different playing levels. A musician usually progresses from one group to another as their skill develops.

Conductor/Director: *Who is in charge?*
The conductor of the group usually places members, selects music, runs rehearsals and conducts performances, although others may also be involved. Find out about the conductor's background. Ask current members of the group about his or her style. Attend a performance or rehearsal. Observe not only how the conductor conducts, but how group members interact with the conductor and with each other.

Requirements: *What is expected of group members?*

Find out what will be expected of group members. Make sure the performance dates and rehearsals fit into your schedule. How much practice is expected between rehearsals? Some performance groups expect that members are also studying with private teachers who will be available to work with them as needed to prepare their music. Find out about fees and other potential expenses for clothing or travel. Some groups also expect members or parents to help raise funds, sell tickets, set up rehearsal space or provide other support.

MUSIC PARENTING

A MUSIC PARENT'S MANY ROLES

A Music Parent plays several important roles in his or her child's music education. The parent provides resources and an environment where musicianship can flourish. The parent provides practical support for musical development, along with encouragement. A Music Parent will take on different roles over time and with different children, but here are some a parent can expect to play.

Resource Provider
Of course, the parent will usually be a major decision-maker in acquiring an instrument, choosing a teacher, identifying performance groups and opportunities, purchasing music and performance apparel, and providing transportation.

Environment Builder
Additionally, parents have a role in providing an environment conducive to the student's musical development. This includes not only a welcoming comfortable physical space for practicing, but also an atmosphere that encourages music-making. Besides setting a favorable tone in the home, the parent can also encourage musical development by cultivating relationships with other musicians,

ranging from accomplished musicians who can provide inspiration to other music students, who can provide fellowship.

Musical Experience Designer
Parents play an important role in exposing their student to different types of music. Most students hear pop, rap and rock music as they go about their everyday activities. Some are exposed to folk songs in elementary school and hymns or gospel music in church. Most, however, will not hear much classical music unless it is intentionally provided. Providing it can be as easy as turning on the classical radio station regularly. Of course, live performances often make a big impression. Seek out opportunities to see and hear skilled musicians of all types in person, making sure the performances and venues are appropriate for your student's age and attention span. Make it a fun experience.

Scheduler
Being a Music Parent requires taking on another set of logistics — scheduling and transporting kids to lessons and rehearsals, as well as clearing the way for practice time. Busy parents may have to juggle this along with their own work and other family needs. Once there is a commitment, though, there's usually a way to work it out. Here are a few tips:
- ♪ **Lesson Times:** In scheduling lesson times, as much as possible, set your student up for a good experience. Consider times when they are apt to be at their best and able to give good attention to their teacher and the musical tasks — when they are not likely to be too tired, hungry or stressed. Also consider your own schedule and when you are best able to get them to the lesson on time without too much stress.
- ♪ **Practice:** The keys to effective practice are regularity and focus. It usually works best to have a regular practice routine. Shorter regular focused practice sessions are better than occasional long or distracted ones. Here, too, consider when the student is

most likely to be able to concentrate well. If possible, give them some choice in when their regular practice times will be and treat it as a scheduled activity.

Practice Coach

While the teacher plays the lead role in teaching students, depending on the teacher, methodology and age of the student, there may be a supporting role for the parent to play. For instance, in the Suzuki method, a parent participates with their young child in a lesson. This allows the parent to work with the child effectively between lessons on the practice tasks that have been assigned. Depending on the age of the child and the situation, a parent might also collaborate with the teacher to figure out the best approach to take with a student both at the lesson and between lessons. Here are some tips for being an effective practice coach:

- ♪ **Partner with the teacher.** Understand what the teacher is trying to accomplish, so that you are able to support the necessary means to get there. Experienced, successful teachers usually follow a specific methodology that has produced results for them. For example, they may break down skills into simple practice tasks and teach them in a certain order to build more complex musical skills. A strings teacher, for instance, may ask the student to practice simple movements in preparation for learning how to play with vibrato. This type of exercise may look or sound strange if you don't know what it's leading up to! Know what the teacher is looking for and building. (If, after understanding it, you disagree with the teacher's methodology in major ways, consider looking for a different teacher.)
- ♪ **Make starting easy.** The hardest part of practicing is overcoming the inertia to begin. Make it easy to start. Keep instruments within easy reach (while protecting them adequately, of course!) Keep recordings of pieces easily accessible. Keep music and materials together where they are easy to find. Keep a practice chart where it is a visible reminder.

- ♪ **Make practice a positive experience.** True progress won't happen without practice, but practice need not be total drudgery. Try to make it fun and engaging. Play games. Present small challenges. Catch students doing something right. Acknowledge progress. Review learning — focus on what the right position looks like or what the right tone sounds like. Use positive language. Resist the urge to criticize — use positive language to redirect the student to try again for the successful result.
- ♪ **Collect questions to ask at the next lesson.**
- ♪ **Provide little rewards to build momentum.** This can range from positive feedback to games to tangible or tasty rewards.

Sounding Board

A parent can help the student sort out issues that come up in the musical journey. By asking thoughtful questions, the parent can guide the student to self-evaluate and make good decisions. For instance, *"What did you like about your playing?"*, *"What advice do you think your teacher would give you?"*, or *"What's your next goal?"*

Fan

As a parent, you're a fan, no matter what. Notice progress. Give authentic compliments. Celebrate. There is a place for critique — usually the role of a teacher — but we all need fans.

Role Model

A parent's example can be a huge influence. If you are learning along with your child, you can be a good role model in your practice habits and responsiveness to your teacher. If you're not currently a music student yourself, you can still be a good role model by exhibiting good practice habits and discipline in any activity.

Caution to parents who are also musicians: You can also be a role model as a musician, however your biggest influence as a role model will show up in your discipline and joy, along, perhaps, with how you use music to make the lives of others better. Be careful not to insist on your child following your exact musical path or style. This can backfire — better to let them find, with your encouragement, their own musical path.

WHEN YOUR YOUNG MUSICIAN WANTS TO QUIT

At some point, your young musician may say he or she wants to quit.

As with learning any worthwhile skill, there are likely to be some difficult points along the way. Typical challenges to sticking with music study include:

- ♪ Competing demands on the student's time
- ♪ Pressure to fit in with non-musician peers
- ♪ Getting to a level that requires a greater commitment of practice or rehearsal time
- ♪ Seeming lack of progress
- ♪ Issues with teachers or music group leaders

When these or any other challenges occur that bring out a possible desire to quit, take a step back. Listen to what the student is saying. Observe a lesson. Talk with the teacher. Think about what the student might be feeling.

Before pulling the plug on music lessons or stopping participation in a music program, consider whether a change of some sort might help. For instance:

- ♪ *Is it time for a change of teacher or director?* Sometimes a fresh approach is needed. Some teachers are particularly good at certain stages, such as for beginning students, or for students who are aiming toward studying music in college. Some teachers are particularly good at certain aspects of music learning — for instance, one teacher might be the right one to help your student develop good technique, while another might inspire their artistic development or specialize in a certain type of music, such as jazz.

♫ *Does the student simply have too much on their plate?* As a student progresses, each step requires a little more from them. Teachers of beginning students might expect 15-30 minutes of daily practice, while an hour or more a day of practice might be needed for an advanced student working on longer and more difficult pieces. More advanced performing groups playing longer and more demanding music typically need longer and more frequent rehearsals. Stress and competing demands from other activities might be a sign that it's necessary to adjust goals and practice expectations or make choices between activities.

♫ *What would it take to spark interest?* When a student has been very interested in music before, but seems to be stuck or to have lost interest, consider what it would take to get them fired up again. Does the student need a new challenge? Would a better or different instrument help? A different performance group and conductor? A different style of music? More fun? Different choices?

♫ *Is it time to reevaluate purpose and goals?* Is the student feeling too much pressure? What's the real purpose for learning music? Is there a way to make it more fun? Sometimes, especially with talented and successful students, in the excitement of competition or with pressure from teachers or conductors, the student's original reasons for wanting to make music are forgotten.

♫ *Is this struggle worth it?* Nearly every music student struggles at some point. He or she reaches a plateau. Getting to the next level requires an upgrade in technique, a greater commitment, or simply more practice time. A little struggle may be a good sign; it is a part of progressing. A huge amount of miserable struggle, though, could signal that it may be time to consider wrapping up formal music lessons.

MUSICAL DEVELOPMENT

LISTENING

Listening is the single most important activity in music. Listening to favorite music is enjoyable, of course. For musicians and music lovers, though, the importance of listening extends much further.

The Importance of Listening

For musicians, listening is important in many ways. Purposeful listening can provide inspiration, accelerate learning and improve musicality.

Inspiration
Listening to accomplished musicians and impressive pieces inspires both beginning musicians in choosing an instrument and more advanced players as they progress. As in any type of learning, it helps to have good role models. Keeping in mind specific pieces you want to be able to play can provide the motivation needed to keep practicing.

Learning
Listening to good players can also accelerate learning. A good recording or live performance provides a model of accuracy of rhythm, pitch and expression. Repeated listening to a piece aids in

memorization. Listening to different players play the same piece provides clues to interpretation and style options.

Musicality

Musicians listen to be able to make fine distinctions in pitch, rhythm and expression. They listen to understand the form and meaning of the music.

Musicians also learn to listen carefully to themselves in order to perfect their playing. They listen carefully to other musicians in their ensemble to blend and to bring out the musical meaning.

Levels of Listening

Musicians learn to listen on many levels.

Sound

The most basic level is listening simply to the sound. On this level, we usually either like or dislike particular music. We may find it relaxing or stimulating, healing or distracting.

Musical Components

Musicians also listen to the musical components. They listen to the different instruments and the part each plays. They listen to the musical form — for themes and their development. They listen to the layers and combinations of instruments or voices and to rhythms, tempo and flow.

Critical Listening

On another level, musicians listen critically. They listen to the playing itself. Is it accurate? Is it artistic? Do the musicians work well together?

Understanding

Lastly, they listen for understanding. On this level, they listen with the composer's ears. For instance, in the era the piece was written, how would it be heard? What did the composer intend? What's the overall meaning of the piece?

Developing Listening

Here are a few tips to develop listening while learning to make music:

1) **Listen to a variety of types of music.** Explore different genres of music by listening to recordings or clips on YouTube. Each genre provides musical elements to expand your listening range. For instance, a classical orchestra provides a huge variety and combination of instruments and sounds. Jazz develops themes through improvisation. World music and different folk genres suggest different types of harmony and rhythm.

2) **Listen to the best.** Look for opportunities to listen to the best players either in performance or on recordings. Listen to lots of good players. Listen for differences in tone, technique and style. This will provide not only inspiration, but can expand your listening and playing range.

3) **Listen with purpose.** As your listening skill develops, you'll be listening more mindfully and hear elements you might not have noticed previously. Try listening to the same piece multiple times listening for different aspects of the music. Listen just to the sound once, then listen to the parts. Listen for form. Then listen critically. Finally, listen for meaning.

4) **Listen to yourself.** Making good music involves good coordination. First, there's the eye-hand coordination between reading and producing a sound. Some instruments require the coordination of playing different notes and techniques with each hand — and even add coordination of the feet.

In the midst of this complex activity, there's another important level of coordination in playing that often gets overlooked — listening as you play. Musicians must coordinate eyes, hands, and feet and then also listen as they play to adjust their playing and interact and balance with other players. While conductors and teachers give their players and students feedback on the sound and suggest adjustments, the best players also learn to listen to themselves as they play.

One effective way to begin to listen to yourself is to record yourself as you play and then listen carefully as you play it back. Listen for accuracy of pitch and rhythm. Listen to the tone and musicality. Listen to the accuracy and balance in coordination of the parts.

Fringe Benefits

Good musical listening carries over to other aspects of life. The capabilities you develop listening as a musician can translate into skillful listening in all sorts of conversations. In conversation, listening on multiple levels involves listening not only to words, but listening to the tone, listening for meaning, listening for patterns and accuracy. Besides listening to the speaker, you listen to yourself and become aware of how you sound to others.

READING MUSIC

Music is meant to be heard. As with spoken language, though, systems have been developed to record musical pieces visually so they can be "read" and reproduced.

Playing "By Ear"

Some musicians play "by ear". That is, they reproduce music from what they have heard, without having to see a visual representation of what others have played. Musicians who play "by ear" generally have a good naturally ability to hear, remember and reproduce music, but most musicians can develop their ability to do this through practice.

Just as we all learned language by hearing, imitating, experimenting and practicing, by exercising the same patience, persistence and willingness to learn through trial-and-error, the majority of musicians can do the same at least to some extent with music. When we learn language, we learn to imitate sounds and then combine those sounds into words. We then learn to combine those words into phrases. As we learn and practice these patterns, putting combinations of sounds and words together become effortless.

With music, we can also learn by listening, imitating, and adjusting until it comes freely. We learn melodies by combining single tones into phrases. We also learn to combine single tones into commonly used patterns, such as scales and chords. As with language, much of this becomes natural with more education and practice. We think of the idea we want to express, and the exact components of language or music flow more freely as we gain more and more experience. Sometimes we imitate others' phrases or repeat our own phrases precisely, but we often "improvise", conveying meaning by combining apt words, sounds or phrases however they come together in the moment.

Reading Music

Most musicians also learn to "read" music. Systems of notation have been developed so that composers can share their music. By understanding how to "read" this notation, other musicians can reproduce musical pieces and play together precisely. A standard system of notation allows musicians from all over the world to understand and play the same music. It allows composers and musicians to communicate and collaborate with each other efficiently.

Elements of Music Notation

To allow musicians to reproduce musical compositions as intended by the composer, music notation includes three main elements: Pitch, Rhythm, and Expression.

Pitch
Musical notation indicates the specific pitch to be played — how "high" or "low" the note sounds. Differences in pitch are perceived by differences in frequency, the speed of sound wave vibrations. The greater the vibrations per second, the higher the pitch.

Musical Development

To indicate the pitch, notes are placed on a "staff" — a set of five parallel lines with four spaces in between them:

A "clef" symbol at the beginning of the staff indicates the general range of the pitch. For instance, notation for medium- and higher-sounding instruments, such as flute, violin, and trumpet, and higher voices — altos and sopranos — is usually written on the "treble clef." Notation for lower-sounding instruments, such as cello, bass, trombone and tuba and lower voices, is usually written on the "bass clef". Pianists read music from a "grand staff", which combines one treble-clef staff, played with the right hand, with a bass-clef staff, played with the left hand. Music for the viola, which has a range in between the treble and bass clef, is written on the "C clef".

Treble clef   Bass clef   C clef

When multiple instruments are being played simultaneously, the parallel staves for each instrument are joined by a vertical bar. While each instrumentalist usually reads from a sheet showing just their own part, the conductor of a group will use a "score" showing all the instruments being played.

Exact pitches are indicated by the vertical placement of note on the staff. They are placed either on the staff lines or in the spaces in between the lines. If a note is lower or higher than the range indicated by the five lines of the staff, extra short lines, called "ledger lines" are added for that single note to show how much higher or lower it sounds.

The pitches are given letter names from the musical alphabet, which goes from A to G and then repeats itself — A, B, C, D, E, F, G, A, B.... When the letter next repeats itself, the relationship to the original pitch is called an "octave". The notes in an octave have vibration frequencies in a 2:1 ratio to each other. That is, the higher note vibrates at exactly twice the frequency of the lower one.

Only seven letter names are used, but there are actually twelve different tones used in Western music, with the extra five falling in between the seven letters. These "in between" tones are indicated with "sharps" and "flats". If the note is slightly higher (a "half-step" or "semitone") than the letter name pitch, a sharp symbol is placed in front of the note: ♯. If the note is a "half-step" lower, a "flat" symbol is placed in front of it: ♭. A "natural" sign cancels a previous sharp or flat sign: ♮.

Every musical piece (except some very contemporary dissonant-sounding pieces) uses one specific tone as a type of harmonic home. The piece is said to be "in the key of" that home tone. Then it uses as many as six other primary related tones. Ordered by pitch, these tones create a "scale". For example, a song in the key of "C" uses the tones C, D, E, F, G, A and B.

Keys other than "C" use tones with sharps or flats. To indicate that a tone is always played a half-step higher or lower throughout a piece of music, a type of musical shorthand is used by placing the sharps or flats at the beginning of every line next to the clef sign. This is called the "key signature". An example would be the key of "D". It would use a scale that includes D, E, F#, G, A, B and C# and the "D" key signature with an F# and C# would be placed at the beginning of every line.

Rhythm

Musical notation also indicates how the notes occur in time.

Notes appear in different shapes to indicate their relative durations. For instance, a "whole" note looks like this: o. A note that lasts half as long, called a "half note" adds a "stem" to look like this ♩ and one that lasts a quarter of the length of time, a "quarter note", fills in the note "head" to look like this: ♩. "Flags" are added to the stems to indicate shorter durations — for example, an "eighth note" uses one flag ♪ and a "sixteenth note" uses two ♬. "Dots" can be attached to any of these to add another half of the note value.

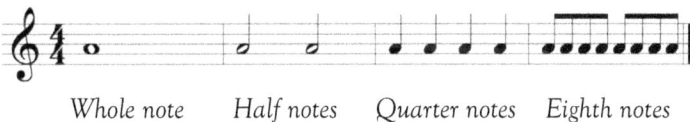

Whole note   Half notes   Quarter notes   Eighth notes

Silence is also an important part of music. Silence is indicated by "rest" symbols that indicate specific relative durations of silence.

Whole rest   Half rests   Quarter rests   Eighth rests

Most musical pieces have a regular "beat". This is indicated at the beginning of the piece through a "time signature". Vertical "bar lines" are placed at regular intervals of the staff throughout a piece of music to divide it into small sections called "measures". The time signature top number shows the number of beats per measure, while the bottom note indicates the type of note that gets one beat.

For example, the first example above indicates that there are three beats per measure, with a quarter note receiving one beat. In the second example, there are four beats per measure, with a quarter note receiving one beat. In the last example, there are six beats per measure with an eighth note receiving one beat.

Additional musical symbols are used to indicate or simplify the format. For instance, some symbols give musical directions, such as the "repeat" sign 𝄇 . The end of a piece is indicated with a "double barline" 𝄁 .

Expression

Lastly, musical notation indicates "how" the music is played.

For instance, dynamics symbols, such as *f* (for "forte", which means "loud" in Italian) or *pp* (for "pianissimo", "quiet" in Italian) indicate how loudly or softly the notes are to be played.

Tempo markings, such as "lento" (slow), "presto" (fast) or "andante" (walking pace) indicate how slowly or quickly a piece is to be played. Sometimes a specific "metronome marking", the number of beats per minute, is shown to indicate the exact speed of a piece.

Musical symbols are also used to indicate articulation, or how the notes are played. For instance, "accent" marks show the musician which notes to bring out: > . A "*staccato*" mark, a dot under or over a note, indicates that it is to be short and detached.

Additional types of musical symbols are used to indicate use of specific techniques. For instance, "*pizz*", meaning "pizzicato", tells string players they should pluck the string instead of using a bow to play it.

Types of Music Notation

When musicians talk about "reading music", they are usually referring to reading the standard music notation used in printed classical music. With this type of notation, music is written out completely and precisely. While this type of notation is almost always used for classical music, other types of music may also employ other methods.

Lead Sheets

For instance, jazz, folk and rock musicians often read from a "lead sheet" or "chart". A lead sheet shows the melody on one staff and then indicates the harmony to be used by chord symbols.

A chord is a combination of notes played together. Chord symbols are a type of musical shorthand. When a musician sees the chord symbol "C", for instance, they know to play a chord or patterns that include the notes C, E and G. Seeing the chord symbol "D7", they know to play a chord or patterns that include D, F#, A and C. With a lead sheet, musicians have some freedom in how they play the harmony part that accompanies the melody. They often use common patterns dictated by the style of music they are playing or the "feel" they want the piece to have. For instance, in a waltz-type song, a folk musician might play a pattern with a single low note followed by two chords (bass-strum-strum, bass-strum-strum). A rock musician might use a familiar "rock" rhythm (bum-bum-ba-bum-ba-dum), while a blues pianist might use a "boogie-woogie" bass pattern. A jazz player will use the notes indicated by the chord symbol as a musical foundation on which to improvise. When multiple musicians are playing together, the chord symbols allow them to play different notes that will harmonize.

Manuscript

Music notation in the composer's handwriting is called "manuscript".

Tablature

Certain instruments may use other types of notation specific to the instrument. For instance, guitarists and lutists may read music from "tablature", a chart showing where to place the fingers on the strings.

PRACTICING

Three factors make a big difference in a music student's progress: Motivation, Guidance, and Practice. (Yes, natural talent helps, but without motivation, good guidance and effective practice, talent alone isn't worth much.)

Motivation, Guidance, Practice

These three success factors are interrelated. If the student is motivated — interested in music, learning to play an instrument they like, playing at least some music that is very appealing to them, has a goal that is both realistic and inspiring, and has good models to provide direction and inspiration — they are more likely to practice. Good guidance from a teacher or learning program shows them what and how to improve by practicing. The progress achieved by good practicing builds success, which increases motivation.

Practice for Results

Practice is essential for making progress. Progress depends on more than just putting the time in on practice, however. It must be effective practice. Effective practice starts with knowing Why, What and How to practice.

Why Practice?: Purpose & Goals

The "why" of music learning will be at least slightly different for every music student. It also may change depending on their age and stage. Keep in mind the overall purpose for learning music. For one student, it may be to prepare for a musical career, while for another it might be to develop enough skill to write and perform their own songs or participate in a music group.

Besides having an overall purpose in learning music, having specific goals for a defined timeframe helps drive progress. Examples of specific goals would be being able to play a specific challenging piece, completing a certain book of pieces or exercises, qualifying for membership in a performing group, or being prepared for a competition or performance.

Whatever the goals are, keep them in the forefront. While a teacher, parent or role model might suggest a goal, it really does work best if the goal is the student's own goal. Intrinsic goals, internally motivated ones, such as a desire to learn, achieve or grow, generally live longer than extrinsic, externally motivated ones, such as winning a prize, impressing another, or avoiding punishment. Don't discount the value of a well-placed bribe from time to time, though. A small incentive can be effective in the short-term and that might just create enough momentum to carry the student forward towards a bigger goal.

What To Practice: Focus

Your teacher or program should be able to give you good guidance on what to practice. (If they don't do this automatically, be sure to ask.)

Music practice generally includes work in several areas:

♪ **Technique:** The foundation of good practice involves learning and reinforcing proper technique (e.g. proper position and movements). For instance, singers learn effective breathing techniques, string players work to develop good bow holds and pianists "curve" their fingers to allow them to play scales rapidly and evenly. While students often find this part of practicing tedious, good technique is essential. Without good technique, players will be limited. It will be too difficult or frustrating to play more difficult pieces and the results will be disappointing. Here are some tips for practicing technique:

- Invest at least a little time every practice session in developing technique. Do this early in your practice session. By paying attention to using and developing good technique for a few minutes at the beginning of your session, you will set yourself up to carry good position and movement through your session.
- Be sure to know exactly what good technique looks, sounds and feels like. Be able to distinguish between doing it "right" and "wrong".

♪ **Musicianship:** Being a good musician requires understanding music principles, reading music well, developing a good "ear" and playing musically.

- **Understanding Music Principles:** Music theory involves learning how music works. Whether the student is reading music or playing by ear, understanding basic principles of music makes playing and memorization easier. This part of the practice session involves learning to recognize and play basic "vocabulary" tools on which music is built — scales, chords and arpeggios (notes of chords played in ascending or descending patterns). It also involves learning to recognize common patterns and forms used in music composition.

- **Reading Music:** Reading music entails understanding the music language and symbols and then developing coordination to be able to quickly produce the indicated sounds accurately. It's looking at printed music and being able to play the correct notes, rhythm and dynamics. The more you do it, the easier it gets. Start with simple patterns and gradually increase the level of difficulty.
- **Listening:** There are several ways to increase musicianship through listening. First, listen to skilled musicians playing the pieces you are learning to play. Listen to get to know the piece. Listen for expression and artistry. Even imagine yourself playing along. Another way to increase musicianship through listening is to develop your "ear" by listening to pieces or parts of pieces and then trying to reproduce them without referring to written music. Start by playing and clapping back rhythms. Sing or play the tune back.
- **Repertoire:** This part of your practice session is devoted to learning pieces. This is often the student's favorite part of the practice session, as it's usually the easiest place to see short-term progress. Depending on the length and difficulty of the pieces, a teacher will typically assign 1-3 at a time. These pieces, or parts of the piece in the case of one longer one, will often be at different stages. For instance, one may be in the initial learning stage of reading the notes and getting the basic coordination down. Another might be in a "polishing" stage, where the student knows the notes and rhythms and is focusing now on details, such as dynamics, and making it more beautiful. Lastly, a student may be memorizing a piece or reviewing earlier pieces to keep them performance-ready.

When working on pieces, the goal should be to:
- ♪ Play using good technique
- ♪ Play the right notes with the right timing and dynamics
- ♪ Play smoothly and evenly
- ♪ Play at the right speed
- ♪ Play musically!

How Long Should I (or My Child) Practice?

The ideal length of a practice period is individual, depending on the student's attention span and goals. A general guideline used by many teachers for their students is:
- ♪ Beginners: 15-30 minutes/day
- ♪ Intermediates: 30-60 minutes/day
- ♪ Advanced: 1 hour +/day

Generally, the more one practices, the more quickly he or she will progress. But quality of practice is what will make the biggest difference.

How To Practice: Using Practice Time Effectively

Mindfulness

Practice is only effective when it is mindful. Mindlessly putting time in on an instrument is actually worse than not practicing at all. It can cause development of bad habits or simply cause frustration, because it is taking time but not producing good results. Good practice requires concentration. Short focused practice is more effective than long distracted or disinterested practice. Take a break if needed.

Focus

Practice should have a specific aim. A good teacher will assign specific practice tasks and help you recognize when you are performing them correctly. To avoid being overwhelmed, work on improving 1-2 things at a time.

Regularity

Regularity is more important than length of practice sessions. Scheduling a regular time for practice improves the likelihood that it will occur. Reasons will come up as to why there's no time to practice. Decide in advance what you will do when that happens. If there's a conflict with your regular time, when will you practice instead? If there's an expectation that missed practice will be rescheduled, it's less likely to be missed.

To get really good at music, as with anything, there's no substitute for putting in the time. (Focused, mindful practice time, of course...) Developing a skill requires concentration and repetition. Often, the hardest part of practicing is getting started. So — just start!

Fun/Flow/Freedom

Consider ways to make practicing more enticing.

- ♪ Make it Fun: Make up games. Use charts, stickers and little rewards for little successes. (This often works well for adults, as well as for young students!)
- ♪ Let It Flow: Vary the types of music and practice activities.
- ♪ Allow Freedom: Give the student some choices about how to practice. For example, let the student pick their practice time and the order of practice tasks.

Feedback

It's important for a student to know when he or she is on the right track. Reinforce good work with specific acknowledgement. One effective way of getting feedback is to keep a recorder or video camera running while practicing and then to play the recording back to check how it looked and sounded.

Techniques For Results

Here are some highly effective music practice techniques:

- ♪ Work on the difficult parts most.
- ♪ Break down challenging sections into small parts to practice separately. For instance, take little chunks and use them as exercises. An effective technique for pianists is to practice parts of a piece with each hand separately.
- ♪ Practice slowly, aiming for evenness and control. Then, using a metronome, gradually increase the speed until it is up to performance speed.
- ♪ When memorizing a piece, practice for "understanding" — that is, don't just rely on "muscle memory" — understand the patterns you are playing.
- ♪ If you are having difficulty with some aspect of a piece, make a note to bring it up with your teacher at your next lesson.

Famous pianist Arthur Schnabel advised parents and teachers not to ask students to "practice". He suggested instead asking *"Have you already made and enjoyed music today? If not — go and make music."*

PERFORMING

If a musician plays and there's no one there to hear it ... does it matter?

Some music students crave an audience, while others dread having to face one. Either way, performing in front of others will be part of most musicians' experience and it can help you grow musically. The mere act of sharing music makes musicians better. We prepare more thoroughly. And music "sounds" different when there are listeners.

For music students, the keys to beneficial performing are: 1) To choose performance opportunities that will be motivating and 2) To develop thinking and practices that will set you up to thrive as a performer.

Performing Opportunities

Built-in Performing Opportunities

Orchestra, band and choir members have built-in performing opportunities with these groups. Members of large musical groups may want to develop their playing skill through solo or small group performing as well.

Private music teachers usually schedule some sort of regular recitals or other performances for their students, but their students may also wish to supplement these with additional solo or group performances.

Small Ensembles

Performing with a few other musicians can be a broadening and fun musical experience. A small group provides a unique musical space where musicians get to collaborate, and at the same time, each individual part makes a big difference.

Small ensemble opportunities can range from a pianist with another instrument or two to a string quartet, rock or bluegrass band or a jazz trio. Some small groups play precisely-written musical arrangements, while others play more improvisationally from "charts" that provide only a melody and chords. Members of small ensembles may also write or arrange music for the group to perform.

Competitions and Festivals

Students may find performing opportunities through competitions or festivals sponsored by music teachers' associations, community music groups or other arts organizations. Preparing for this type of performance can provide motivation to perfect pieces.

Solo and ensemble "festivals" provide an opportunity for students to play in front of a guest music teacher who gives feedback and suggestions on their playing, along with a "rating". Since different teachers focus on different aspects of playing, this can be a good learning opportunity.

Some organizations put on competitions for music students that offer prizes that range from scholarships to opportunities to perform with an orchestra. These types of events are usually organized by age or skill level and require the student to play certain types of pieces or even specific pieces. If preparing for one of these, find out the details well in advance. Most give a specific time limit for pieces and some include other elements, such as playing scales, as well.

Clubs, Coffeehouses and "Open Mics"
Some establishments or clubs sponsor events when any performer can sign up to play a number or two. This can be a fun way to try out new material and get performance experience in a low-key setting.

Retirement Homes
Retirement homes often welcome performers, including young people.

Family and Friends
Family and friends normally enjoy shared music in small doses.

What About Reluctant Performers?
Performing can be beneficial for music students even when it's not for a big crowd. Consider the size and type of audience that feels best. A reluctant performer may feel happiest just playing for one or two close encouraging friends or family members. (Don't limit them unnecessarily, though. They may also enjoy sharing their music at a retirement home, because there they are not just playing music, they are brightening someone's day.)

On the other hand, some musicians are happiest just playing for themselves to relax and enjoy the music for its own sake.

Note for Parents: It's fine to gently encourage your child to perform in appropriate situations, but take your cues from him or her. Avoid putting your child on the spot or forcing a reluctant performer. Also, be aware of your own signs so that you aren't inadvertently making your child nervous or upset through body language or facial expressions that convey pressure, nervousness or criticism.

Thriving As a Performer

It does get easier.
For some, performing feels very natural. One of the many benefits of starting music early with the Suzuki method is that from the

beginning, students perform often with and in front of each other and low-key audiences. They never develop a fear of performing, because it seems quite natural.

Many people, though — especially adults — have some fear about performing in front of others. As with most things, it usually gets easier the more you do it. Whether you're a natural performer or a reluctant one, here are some performing techniques and ideas to ease your way:

Perform with joy!

How do you think about performing? Those who dread it often view performing as an obligation to play perfectly and avoid humiliating oneself in front of others, while those who thrive on it more likely see it as an opportunity to share what they love.

It usually boils down to an underlying feeling of one of two things — pressure or joy. Pressure comes from feeling you need to impress others. Pressure is really just a symptom of fear — fear of making mistakes, or not being well thought-of, or not being as good as others.

On the other hand, embracing the opportunity to perform with joy produces an entirely different experience. It can be the joy of sharing the beauty or excitement of the music. It can be the joy of sharing unique individual expression or evidence of progress.

How could you shift your thinking about performing from pressure to joy?

Prepare

Before stepping out to perform in front of others, prepare your music and prepare yourself.

There is no substitute for preparing your music well. You must know it well and practice it until it flows easily. If you can't play it well in practice, it's highly unlikely that you'll play it well in performance. If you plan to play from memory, be sure you really know the music — understand the form and know the order. Practice starting from different points in the music. Sometimes musicians think they know a piece from memory, but it is only surface memory — memory their muscles have developed as habit — and if they get interrupted, they can't find their place.

Also prepare yourself by getting into a state of mind conducive for delivering a good performance. Performers often spend a few minutes before a performance by themselves relaxing and concentrating. Some even work their big muscles behind stage to knock out some nervousness. Relax. Breathe. Envision how you want the first few measures to go.

Don't worry about mistakes.
If you have prepared well, you probably won't make any. If you do, keep going and it's likely that the majority of listeners won't even know. And even if they do, unless you're in a high-stakes competition or an audition for Juilliard, it won't matter. The music itself keeps moving and most of the audience will walk away, not with the memory of a single note or sound, but with an overall feeling. Part of the excitement of live performance is the element of unpredictability. The music comes out a little differently each time. Resist the temptation to think about your mistake during the rest of the performance. Be musical, keep moving and focus on each new moment.

Don't compare yourself to others.
(Translation for Parents: Don't compare your kid to other kids or yourself to other parents.) Enjoy listening to masters. Know that they have devoted thousands of hours to developing their skill. Enjoy listening to your peers. Rejoice in their progress. If you currently are more advanced than others you hear, look up and realize there's always someone else more advanced than you are. There's always room to improve.

Each musician comes with his or her own special combination of gifts, strengths, style, experience, goals and challenges. Some are excellent technicians. Others excel at connecting with their audience.

Some aspire to soloist status, while others are happy to sing in the choir. Some love and are best suited to classical music. Others love jazz and can improvise.

If you find yourself secretly or not-so-secretly envious of someone else's skill, consider what they may have had to do to develop it. Use that as fuel to move toward doing what it takes to get to a higher level of musical skill. Or just enjoy where you are, recognizing the sacrifices needed to reach a very high skill level.

Choose a fitting performance venue.

The space you perform in, the musicians you perform with and the audience you perform for will all affect your comfort level. Choose each of these with your goals in mind. For a beginner or a musician who hasn't yet overcome nervousness in performing, a low-key venue with a small, friendly audience is best. Later, performing for a bigger audience or with higher-level performers may be motivating. Work up to bigger performance challenges as your skill and confidence develop. It usually works well to challenge yourself a little bit, but not excessively. As with other aspects of music learning, stretch, not stress, works best.

Focus

While you are performing, stay totally focused on making music. Shut out other thoughts — fear, distractions, worries about criticism. Be alert to the other musicians. Stay in the moment.

MUSICAL PROGRESS: REVISITING YOUR PURPOSE AND GOALS

Musical progress takes place gradually. Sometime there are big leaps when you suddenly "get" a major concept (*Oh, that's how a major chord is constructed!*) or a technique falls in place (*Oh! I get how a correct vibrato feels! I can do it!*). Mostly, though, progress takes place in small ways in every good practice session and through every performance along the way. You are constantly building technique, skill and repertoire. If you aren't specifically looking for it, though, you may not notice how far you've come.

At some point, it will be time to revisit your Musical Learning Purpose and Goals. Stand back and take stock of your progress. Think back over the last year (or however long it's been since you last took stock), and consider:

♪ *What's different and better than before?*
♪ *Which goals have I reached?*
♪ *What practice techniques have worked well for me?*
♪ *What have I enjoyed?*
♪ *What has inspired me?*
♪ *What, if anything, has been frustrating?*
♪ *What discoveries have I made?*

If you have recorded yourself playing in the past, record yourself again and notice the difference.

Then consider what you want for yourself going forward. Ask yourself:

- ♪ *Do I still have the same overall Musical Learning Purpose? If not, what is it now?*
- ♪ *How are things going with my teacher(s)? If my purpose, interests or needs have changed, have I discussed it with them? Is that teacher still a good fit for me?*
- ♪ *How are things going in my performing groups? Are they still a good fit? What new performing opportunities do I want to pursue?*
- ♪ *What new music would I like to learn?*
- ♪ *What aspects of my musicianship would I like to improve?*
- ♪ *Am I devoting the amount of time I'd like to focused practice? If not, what adjustments could I make?*
- ♪ *What new Music Learning Goals will I set for myself?*

Now, write down your updated purpose and goals:

My Musical Learning Purpose:

I want to learn to make music because...

My Music Learning Goals:

My current goals are to...

Specifically, I will...(do what) by...(when).

Also, consider your learning processes: how you are working with your teachers, how you are using your practice and rehearsal time, how you are contributing to performance groups and your performance experiences:

- ♪ *What would you like to do more often?*
- ♪ *What would you like to do less often?*
- ♪ *What changes, if any, would be productive?*
- ♪ *What changes will you make?*

It's useful to go through this self-evaluation process every now and then. It may also be helpful to get feedback and suggestions from your teachers, conductors and other musical learning partners. In music, there's always more to learn.

Lastly, don't forget to celebrate your progress and enjoy playing and sharing your music with others!

MUSIC AND CAREERS: THE OBVIOUS AND NOT-SO-OBVIOUS

When people first think of music and careers, they are likely to focus on the most visible music careers – those that involve performing.

Music Performance Careers
Top-level classical performers may be found performing as soloists, in orchestras, opera companies or other musical ensembles. These professional positions are scarce, demanding, and very competitive.

Skilled performers also find performance opportunities playing in recording studios, as church musicians and as freelance performers. Freelancers are hired as soloists, ensemble members or supplemental musicians for groups for concerts, studio recording, shows and events.

Classical music careers require not only talent, but great motivation and discipline. Serious classical musicians typically start preparing very early for their careers and make tradeoffs in lifestyle in order to do what they love. While a few do well financially, most could be considered underpaid considering the relative level of preparation, skill and work required. Few outside of these careers truly understand the focus, discipline, and persistence required.

Performance career demands in other genres of music are similar in many ways. Although jazz, pop, rock, folk, blues, country or other types of performers may have less formal training or may not have begun their musical training as early as classical pros, developing performance-level skill in these areas also requires great motivation and persistence.

Being a skilled, hardworking musician is just the start in these careers, though. Success usually also requires marketing and business skill. While a few fortunate performers have regular positions, most performers must constantly be promoting themselves looking for and creating musical opportunities. A few can afford to pay agents, promoters or business managers, but most must, at least in the beginning, promote themselves. Making a good living likely requires not only musical skill, but skill in relationship-building, communication, negotiation, promotion and administration.

Careers in Music Education

Musicians who also enjoy teaching can find very satisfying careers as music educators either in schools or private studios. Here, too, along with musical skill, teachers must have good interpersonal, communication and administrative skill. Public school and some other types of teaching positions require a music or music education degree.

Creative and Business Careers

Musicians with special skills in composing, conducting, arranging, recording or producing can pursue careers in these areas.

Musicians who also develop skills in business and marketing may use that combination for careers in the entertainment industry and music-related businesses and organizations.

Any Career

What may not be so obvious is that no matter which career one pursues, a background in music can be helpful in many ways. Many of the qualities and skills one develops in learning music can carry over to bolster success in any career. For instance:

- ♪ **Discipline:** Successful musicians develop self-motivation and effective work habits. They learn to prepare, to work out the details and to persist.
- ♪ **Performance:** In learning to perform for audiences, musicians develop poise, concentration and confidence.
- ♪ **Teamwork:** Musicians not only learn to perform as individuals, but also how to be effective team members. In performance groups, they learn to support other team members and deliver reliable performance, to recognize when to stand out and when to blend in and to adapt to different leaders.
- ♪ **Listening:** Musicians learn to listen deeply. They learn to listen on multiple levels — for accuracy, for meaning, for themes, for tone and for blend.
- ♪ **Creativity:** Composers and arrangers, of course, develop obvious creative skills. Jazz musicians learn to improvise. But through exposure to different types and pieces of music, all musicians pick up processes and ideas that open thinking to creativity in any field.

Success

You might be surprised to find the number and variety of successful people in fields other than music who also have musical backgrounds.

For instance, several U.S. Presidents have also been musicians. Thomas Jefferson, a skilled violinist, also played cello and clavichord. Harry Truman and Richard Nixon were both accomplished pianists. During his 1992 run for President, Bill Clinton's popularity increased after he played saxophone with the house band on the Arsenio Hall Show.

Some of the world's most famous scientists and inventors were also musicians. Einstein once said that if had not been a scientist, he would have been a musician, noting "I know that the most joy in my life has come to me from my violin." Benjamin Franklin composed music, played several instruments and also invented an instrument known as the "glass armonica".

No matter what career you choose to pursue, the experience of learning music will carry many benefits.

MUSICAL LIVES

Whether you are an adult wanting to enrich your own life with music or a parent wanting to give your child a good musical foundation, musical experience adds a special dimension to life.

Making Music Makes Life Better
Whoever, whenever and wherever you are in life, music makes it better. Music offers beauty, energy, and inspiration. Music offers a path to develop character, confidence and creativity. Music offers a means like no other for collaboration and connection.

Music lets us rise above our everyday troubles. In a workshop on using harps in healing, one of my classmates spoke about how playing the harp for himself every day gave him relief from a painful physical condition. I've known more than a few doctors who play for an hour or two to relax after finishing their long shifts, as well as many others who enjoy playing as a means of escaping to another realm. As the Mexican proverb goes, *"Quien canta, sus males espanta."* *("He who sings drives his worries away.")*

Music lets us experience higher levels of humanity. It enables us to experience and become proficient in multiple dimensions. It involves both our senses and intuition, intellect and emotion, the perceptible and the invisible. We experience it in time and space and connection with others.

> "Music conveys messages from heart to heart." – Beethoven

In studying and practicing music, students often acquire rich side benefits, such as increased concentration, self-confidence and listening skill. Researchers have found that listening to music and playing music can even make us "smarter", in terms of improved SAT scores and (at least temporarily) IQ points.

Music lets us experience deep special connections with others. Whether through the rhythms of rock, the spontaneity of jazz improvisation, or the rich sounds of an orchestra, musicians experience a special connection like the one Garrison Keillor describes so beautifully of choral singers:

> "To sing like this, in the company of other souls, and to make those consonants slip out so easily and in unison, and to make those chords, so rich that they bring tears to your eyes. This is transcendence. This is the power that choral singing has that other music can only dream of."
>
> – Garrison Keillor

Music In The Air

One doesn't need to be a music professional to catch a glimpse of this. One of the delights of music is that it can be enjoyed by anyone. Over the years, some of my favorite music students were adults with sincere, modest goals, such as the woman who came to me for voice lessons "so that I won't sound like Edith Bunker (from the TV show *All in the Family*) all my life." She simply enjoyed singing along more beautifully on hymns at church.

Music is always there for you. You can begin making music any time and return anytime.

> "My idea is that there is music in the air; the world is full of it, and you simply take as much as you require." – Sir Edward Elgar

A musician will never be bored. There is always more music to hear, to learn and to compose. Any musician can always become a better listener, player and ensemble member. There are always new discoveries to be made in the music, new combinations, instruments, and genres to explore. As with mothers, a musician's work is never done. The opportunities are limitless.

Think Of Yourself Musically
No matter what your age, stage, background, or profession, you can be a musician. If you are thinking, *well, I'm not really a musician, I'm not very good*, consider this: It's not about proficiency, it's about attitude.

I clearly remember a musically-defining moment during a community choral group rehearsal years ago. Even during our warm-ups, our new director referred to us as "singers". The group consisted of a broad range of singers — some professionals and semi-professionals, some talented and experienced amateurs, and some music lovers fairly new to singing. Even the more experienced among us may not really have thought of ourselves explicitly before as "singers". An interesting thing happened when he referred to us this way. We all sat up a bit straighter, were more alert to our breathing, vowels and cutoffs, listened to each other more closely to perfect our blend, and sang more expressively.

Similarly, I remember a piano teacher who promoted musicality by calling her students "musicians" instead of only "pianists". Pianists often play by themselves and can get bogged down in the challenge of trying to coordinate the movements of two hands, a foot, and multiple fingers. By encouraging us to listen as we played, to understand the historical context of the music we played and to communicate through our playing, she activated our musicianship.

How would things change if you thought of yourself as "a musician"? (Yes, you.) No matter where you are in your musical journey and whatever roles you play in life, try this. Even if you only play for yourself, thinking of yourself as a musician will transform your experience.

Which Musical Roles Will You Play?

As you think of yourself musically, don't limit yourself to thinking of being a musician as simply being a singer or player of a particular instrument. There are so many roles a musician can play – connector, creator, communicator, inspirer. And don't forget the all-important musical roles of listener, supporter and fan.

Similarly, don't limit yourself to one type of music. While you are likely to develop preferences and focus on the type of music that fits you best, there is much to learn from different musical genres. For instance, studying classical music can provide a good foundation in technique, principles of harmony and form. Exploring jazz can open up new musical worlds via improvisation and collaboration. Folk, rock and other popular forms of music tell stories, create energy, inspire movement and unite people in causes and action. Music from different parts of the world extends our concepts of rhythm, instrumentation and harmony.

Enjoy Your Musical Life

I hope you have found this book helpful as you begin or continue your musical life or encourage a child or someone else in theirs.

Those who choose musical lives, along with their other roles in life, take on an exciting lifelong journey. As we practice and experience more music, we often hear and understand more about it – about what has always been there. Even the most accomplished musicians are always learning and making new musical discoveries.

Through our musical lives, we may also experience and understand more in a greater sense of life. As we progress musically, we may increasingly recognize new aspects of beauty and harmony, individuality and unity, order and creativity, love and life.

Wishing you a fulfilling musical life!

RECOMMENDED BOOKS

Talent Development and Music Education

Nurtured By Love **or** *Talent Development From Age Zero*, Dr. Shinichi Suzuki

These two similar short books by Dr. Shinichi Suzuki, the founder of The Suzuki Method, illustrate his philosophy and method of "Talent Education". According to Dr. Suzuki, all children have great potential that can be nurtured and developed. In these books, Suzuki shows parents how to create an environment to encourage both development of musical skill and beautiful character. Either of these books provide an inspiring easy read parents may find enlightening even beyond the realm of music education.

The Talent Code, Daniel Coyle

According to author Coyle, "Greatness isn't born. It's grown" through deep practice and motivation, along with skillful coaching. Coyle combines brain and behavioral research with illustrations of hotbeds of significant talent development showing how principles of practice, motivation and coaching apply in athletics, music, intellectual and other pursuits.

A Whole New Mind, Daniel Pink

Futurist Daniel Pink writes about how creativity and "right-brain" skills and abilities will rule in this age, now that computers can perform many of the functions that led to success in the past.

The Art of Possibility, Rosamund Stone Zander and Benjamin Zander

This book outlines a dozen practices for breakthrough creativity. Check out "Giving an A", which describes conductor and professor Benjamin Zander's approach to teaching, grading and developing talent at the New England Conservatory of Music.

The Inner Game of Music, Barry Green with Timothy Gallwey

Bassist Barry Green joined with Timothy Gallwey, author of *The Inner Game of Tennis*, to apply the principles of "natural learning" to music. Their advice will help musicians improve performance by reducing mental interference and improving awareness and concentration.

The Music Lesson: A Spiritual Search For Growth Through Music, Victor L. Wooten

Through a fictional story, Grammy Award-winning bassist Victor L. Wooten shares lessons and ideas about music and life.

Changing Lives: Gustavo Dudamel, El Sistema, and the Transformative Power of Music, Tricia Tunstall

In this inspiring book, Tunstall shows how music can transform lives through the story of Los Angeles Philharmonic's young conductor, Gustavo Dudamel, and the Venezuelan music education program that gave him his start. The El Sistema program aims to rescue children from the depredations of poverty by providing 370,000 young Venezuelans with instruments, instruction and hope.

Recommended Books

Healing At The Speed of Sound: How What We Hear Transforms Our Brains and Our Lives, Don Campbell and Alex Doman

Don Campbell, author of *The Mozart Effect*, and Alex Doman, a specialist in the practical application of sound, show how music, sound and silence can affect how we feel and function. The book includes research on brain science and the effects of sound, as well as suggestions on how to use music to improve your life. Besides addressing the effects of sound on healing and aging, the book illustrates many benefits of music education – from improvements in SAT scores to increases in self-confidence. In an era of mindless noise exposure and pollution, the authors also encourage readers to purposefully create their own "sound diet".

This is Your Brain On Music: The Science of a Human Obsession, Daniel J. Levitin

In this unusual and interesting book, musician and neuroscientist Levitin explores the connections between science and music, from the foundations of music theory to why we like certain types of music.

You Can Read Music, Amy Appleby

This book covers the basics of music notation, including clefs, pitches, rhythm, key signatures and expression. It also provides an explanation of chords and chord charts for piano and guitar. A CD with audio examples and exercises that complement the text is included.

Free Play: Improvisation in Life and Art, Stephen Nachmanovitch

In this book about improvisation and the creative process, Nachmanovitch explores concepts such as surrender, the importance of practice and play, and the power of limits and mistakes.

The Listening Book: Discovering Your Own Music, W. A. Mathieu

This delightful collection of short essays and exercises explores sound, music and the power of listening.

Music Genres and Composers

Inside Music, Karl Haas

Excellent classical music reference book written by the creator and host of *Adventures in Good Music*. In a readable, entertaining way, Haas covers topics such as "music's main ingredients", instruments, the orchestra, music history and musical forms.

Young People's Concerts, Leonard Bernstein

Between 1958 and 1978, conductor and composer Leonard Bernstein presented 53 televised concerts for young people with the New York Philharmonic orchestra. His mission was to help them understand the language of music and to encourage them become active listeners. In these concerts, Bernstein answers big musical questions, such as "What Does Music Mean?", "What is Classical Music?" and "What is Orchestration?", as well as exploring "Humor in Music" and different musical forms. Both a collection of lectures in book form and concert DVDs are available.

Bach, Beethoven and the Boys, David W. Barber

A humorous human look at music history to supplement the serious, detailed, academic ones.

Spiritual Lives of Great Composers, Patrick Kavanaugh

In this book, Kavanaugh shows us a different aspect of the lives of 20 musical masters, going beyond the standard historical and musical details to reveal the spiritual views that inspired them. Along with short biographies illustrated by the composers' personal conversations and writings, listening recommendations are included for each.

Beethoven Lives Upstairs, Barbara Nichol and Walter Babiak

This CD tells the story of Beethoven and his music from the perspective of a young boy living downstairs, incorporating excerpts from many of Beethoven's best-known works. It is from the award-winning Classical Kids series, which also includes the stories of Bach, Handel, Mozart, Vivaldi and Tchaikovsky.

What To Listen For In Music, Aaron Copland

In this classic book, composer Aaron Copland writes about how we listen, explores the basic elements of music — rhythm, melody, harmony and tone color — and explains musical forms.

The NPR Curious Listener's Guide to American Folk, Kip Lornell

In this book, Lornell explores the types of music folklorist Mike Seeger once described as "All the music that fits between the cracks" — ballads, blues, bluegrass, Cajun, cowboy, klezmer, gospel, protest music and such. He not only explores the history and different styles of folk music, but also provides short biographies of influential performers, a discussion of significant songs, a glossary of folk music terms and a list of recommended CDs and resources. It provides a good starting-point for listening and exploring a range of traditional "grass roots" musical styles. National Public Radio has also produced several other "Curious Listener's Guides" to other types of music, such as blues, Celtic music and world music.

Rise Up Singing: The Group Singing Songbook, Peter Blood and Annie Patterson

Lyrics and chords for 1,200 folk songs.

What Jazz Is: An Insider's Guide to Understanding and Listening To Jazz, Jonny King

Jazz pianist Jonny King explains how jazz works — what improvisation means, what to listen for and how different instruments are used. He also discusses what's important and distinctive in the playing styles of famous jazz musicians and selects ten recordings to illustrate different styles.

Jazz: An Introduction to the History and Legends Behind America's Music, Bob Blumenthal

An introduction to jazz organized by era, including photos, facts and listening suggestions.

About the Author

Music has always been an important part of author Jane Moyer's life. She started playing the recorder in 2nd grade, begged her mother for piano lessons in 3rd, joined the band in 4th and has never been without a song in her heart, head and fingers since.

After laying a strong foundation in classical music by earning a Bachelor of Music degree at Michigan State University, Jane expanded her musical life by exploring jazz and playing folk music out in the real world. She's learned to play ten different musical instruments. While working in business and talent development careers, Jane has enjoyed a parallel part-time career as a professional musician, as well as playing and singing with friends and family.

Jane has played many musical roles — from formally-taught to self-taught music student, performer, teacher, arranger, accompanist, ensemble member, music spouse and parent. She's picked up musical ideas by hanging around conservatory students, church musicians, folkies, jazz cats, opera buffs, Suzuki music teachers, composers and songwriters. She takes in used instruments and gives them a good home as others might take in stray cats.

Jane is grateful to her patient musical husband, many wonderful music teachers and role models, and her parents, who not only were loving caretakers and good role models, but paid for all of those piano and voice lessons — even when she didn't practice.

www.ingramcontent.com/pod-product-compliance
Lightning Source LLC
LaVergne TN
LVHW051832080426
835512LV00018B/2840